the norse tarot

THE
NORSE
TAROT

GODS, SAGAS AND RUNES FROM THE LIVES OF THE VIKINGS

CLIVE BARRETT

Aquarian
An Imprint of HarperCollins*Publishers*

The Aquarian Press
An Imprint of HarperCollins*Publishers*
77–85 Fulham Palace Road,
Hammersmith, London W6 8JB

Published by The Aquarian Press 1989
7 9 10 8 6

A catalogue record for this book
is available from the British Library

ISBN 0 85030 726 0

Typeset by Harper Phototypesetters Limited,
Northampton
Printed in Great Britain by
Woolnough Bookbinding Limited,
Irthlingborough, Northamptonshire

CONTENTS

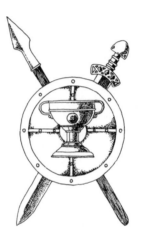

CHAPTER 1

INTRODUCTION AND BACKGROUND TO THE NORSE TAROT

Life is the search for that which is lost, for we each have within us our own personal quest. What we seek is unknown to us, but still we strive onwards. Our aims, even though we are not conciously aware of them, have a great effect on our lives, governing the way we think and the actions we take. Each of them personal, individual and indefinable.

The difficulty in expressing and explaining the search has resulted in the generation of much of the mythology of the past, producing many varied and diverse relatings of what is basically the same story. Over and over again, it is repeated throughout history. The theme, beneath its constantly changing trappings, always remains the same. Each an attempt by an individual, or a group, to describe the indescribable quest, each a reflection, and only a reflection, of the urge to know the unknowable.

We are all looking for something that we cannot explain; perhaps we are not even aware that there is anything lost, but still we go on, searching blindly.

The goal has been variously described as the Philosophers Stone, Immortality, Oneness with Nature, Perfection, the Truth and the Grail. The search is looked on as the Great Work, the Way, the Path to Righteousness. All philosophers seek the same end — only the terminologies are different. This difference in terminology leads to misunderstanding between the varying belief systems, which is most regrettable as each is driven by the same internal force.

The pattern of the search is cyclic. One starts at the beginning and progresses, only to return to the point of origin.

It is the cycle seen in the sun, progressing through the hours of the day and the seasons of the year. The sun rises in the morning, growing steadily towards midday and the time of its greatest strength, then moves on to its glorious ending at sunset, where it will rest through the night. Through the seasons, the sun follows its course from winter to summer, and back to winter again. It is the cycle of the moon as it passes through the month, waxing and waning, new moon to old moon.

The search is illustrated perfectly in the Major Arcana of the Tarot — the Fool begins his adventure with no knowledge of what is to come. In human form he is the very essence of inexperience. Moving through the cards he gains knowledge and wisdom, understanding and compassion; he experiences the heights of joy and the depths of despair. Ultimately he sheds his earthly pleasures and attributes to reach perfection and completion.

But just what *does* he achieve? Not only his method, but also his final achievement is veiled in mystery, open to a mixed and varied interpretation.

The origins of the Tarot may well have been implicit within the very first orally transmitted tales, perhaps predating even the earliest civilizations. For beneath the surface of the Tarot, a framework can be found upon which the majority of cyclic legends were formulated.

The number of comparisons that can be made between the story told in the Cards of the Tarot's Major Arcana and

the myths and legends of the past is remarkable. From Sumerian times and the legend of Bel (Baal) to the biblical life of Christ, the same concepts constantly repeat themselves. To take an example, extreme at first sight: in the present day version of the legend of Robin Hood there are many areas of close correspondence with the Tarot, but when one considers that the tales of Robin Hood have their roots in mythology, the reason at once becomes clear.

Among the story-tellers of the past, the same tale was told in a multitude of forms. It was the story of a beautiful and perfect god — his name was Osiris, Mithrah, or Arthur. The story told of his life and how he was loved by all; it told of his death that was mourned by all; and it told of his resurrection that would bring joy to the world.

The northern poets told the story of Balder. The god of the Sun and the child of Odin. They told how he came amongst the gods of Asgard and won their hearts, the way that he was killed by the cruel treachery of Loki, and how, after the destruction of the gods at Ragnarok, he returned to a refreshed and welcoming earth.

THE NORSE PEOPLES

In the year 793, Viking raiders sacked the monastery at Lindisfarne, and for the next three hundred years Vikings held considerable influence over the Western world.

The name *Viking* is of unknown origin; many roots have been suggested but none with certainty. It is used, however, as a collective name for the people of Denmark, Norway and Sweden, and later of Iceland. Throughout the period, their activities were prompted by a number of factors.

The most important of these were the excellent ships available and the rising population of the Scandinavian countries. The land was never highly productive and the time came when it could no longer sustain its people. The custom of passing the ownership of farmsteads to the eldest son left an increasing number of younger sons with no land to call their own and no hope of finding any within the country of their fathers. As a result they sought their fortunes elsewhere. Sailing overseas they took the many dangers and uncertainties in their stride. As merchants, settlers or pirates, they would use their proven ship-building and navigational skills to try their luck in foreign lands.

Their acheivements were considerable. Using the rocky island chains of the North Sea as stepping stones, they progressed from the Shetland Isles to the Orkneys and Hebrides. From there they colonized Scotland and the Scottish Isles, Ireland, the Isle of Man and the north and east of England. They also settled in large areas of France and Spain — Normandy is named after them and Russia takes her name from the *Rus*, the Swedish Vikings. Travelling via their colonies in Iceland and Greenland they reached the American continent. A short lived settlement was established, some time around the year 1000, in Newfoundland, known to the Vikings as Vinland.

Their great success was due in no small part to their aggressive spirit and their defiant attitude towards death. They had a deep-seated sense of resignation to the hardness of life. The world was a cruel place in which to live, as they well knew, but they refused to be intimidated by its ways, even to the point of laughing in the face of death.

The myths and sagas that have been passed down to us bear out this attitude, reflecting as they do an acceptance of eventual certainty of defeat at the hands of fate.

Even the gods were mortal: without the rejuvenatory powers of the Idun's apples they too would have soon succumbed to the passage of time. Nor were the gods considered to be all-powerful. They had no more control over their final downfall than had the average man — perhaps, even, they had less.

The myths of the Vikings were not however theirs alone. They represented the northern edge of a people of similar beliefs covering the whole of Europe. From before the time of the Romans to the end of the Viking period and on, the same gods had captured the minds of man. There were regional differences; the Teutonic tribes referred to Wotan, whilst in England his name was Odin, although the gods themselves remained the same.

By the time of the first Viking raids on the British Isles, however, the population was, nominally at least, Christian. The Ancient Britains (i.e. the British Celts) had been converted to Christianity before the departure of the Romans early in the fifth century. But from about 450, following the various invasions of Angles, Saxons and Jutes, they reverted

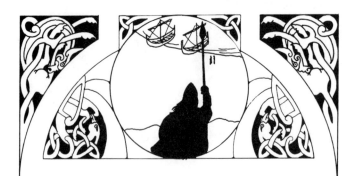

back to their former state of paganism.

However, the Celts of Cornwall, Wales, Scotland and Ireland remained Christian. The Celtic Church flourished in these areas. Contact with these kingdoms, combined with the activities of the Celtic missionaries, persuaded the Anglo-Saxons to become Christians themselves. By the time of the Sinod of Whitby in 663, the whole of Britain was, for the second time, Christian. Hence the outrage expressed in the *Anglo-Saxon Chronicle's* entry for the year 793. The Vikings had not only sacked the Monastery at Lindisfarne, they had brought back the old gods. After an absence of 130 years in England, and even longer in the rest of the British Isles, paganism had returned.

The final Viking invasion of Britain came in 1066. In that year Harold Hardrada, one of the most renouned men of his time, arrived with a mighty host on the shores of northern England. Sailing up the waters of the Ouse, he was joined by many sympathetic Norsemen from the area. leaving their ships behind, they marched on York. On a bright sunny day, at the river crossing of Stamford Bridge, they were met and defeated by the English army under its leader, the Saxon king Harold Godwinson. Following their victory the English marched south and were themselves defeated at Hastings by an army also of Nordic descent, the Normans.

Throughout the period of their dominance, their social structure remained fairly stable. It consisted of an upper warrior class and the lower peasant class. The warriors, or earls were farmers in peace time, and those of them who were away from home during the summer months, generally

returned to their farmstead for the winter. They worshipped the god Odin as the god of war. Believing that half their number, on failing in battle, would go to his hall *Valhalla* to enjoy a perpetual cycle of fighting and merry-making. The other half would go to the hall of Odin's wife Freya, where they would be joined by their own faithful wives and loved ones.

The peasants worked the land as smallholders. They saw Thor as their protector, for he was the god of the ordinary man, a god that common people could identify with. In his palace of Bilskinir, he welcomed them as their masters were welcomed in Valhalla.

Whatever a man's rank, a wide range of skills were necessary for his survival. Some were farmers, so knowledge of all aspects of farming was required, from working the land to breeding stock. If conditions allowed, they would also be fishermen, and would be highly proficient in boat-building as well as seamanship. In addition, a man would make furniture, tools, and all his fishing equipment, using wood, leather, metal and any other material that came to hand.

The women too were expected to provide various necessities. They did the spinning and weaving, the milking and butter making, as well as bringing up the children. They were considered the head of the household, and kept the keys of the house suspended from their belts. Together the family produced and manufactured all its requirements.

The family unit was considered to be the most important aspect of life. Besides being self-sufficient it would provide help in times of trouble. Individual members would gather

together to support each other whenever the need arose — to their deaths if necessary. To extend the benefits of mutual aid further, friendship between family groups was promoted whenever possible. Loyalty to one's family and friends was the highest of all virtues; the more people a man was able to depend upon in times of need, the safer his position would be.

This did of course necessitate a rigid set of laws to prevent family feuds growing out of hand. Providing set amounts of compensation for various acts and misdeeds, the offender could also be pronounced an outlaw, which meant not only that he was literally beyond the protection of the law, but also had the effect that any wrong done to him could not be legally redressed by his family or friends.

THE RUNES

Runes are generally accepted to have been in use about the year 300 BC. Their origin is unknown, but it is likely that they derive from two main sources. Firstly from magical symbols already in use, and secondly borrowings from alphabets to which the northern peoples had contact. The runes *Cen, Rad* and *Is* clearly fall into this second category.

The rune figures were designed for cutting into wood; using a sharp knife, the straight lines cut easily across the grain. The message would be read along the length of the

wood. To do otherwise would mean cutting with the grain, and so risk losing some of the clarity. Stone inscriptions came later and show evidence of a rounding of the individual forms, this medium not presenting the same limitations as wood.

The runes were used for a variety of purposes, from talismanic inscriptions to name tags for marking one's purchases at the market until they could be collected. That they were used in some way for divination cannot be doubted, but in precisely what fashion we do not know. However it would be incorrect to assume that the use of runes was feared or suppressed by the Church, as ecclesiastical inscriptions using a mixture of Roman script and runes, at times within the same word, are extant. Also it seems that the carvers of many inscriptions were equally at home with either form.

The runic alphabet, called a futhark or futhork (after the first six letters), changed many times in its period of use, alternative forms existing simultaneously. As knowledge of the runes passed from place to place, its general form would be adjusted to suit the local differences in pronunciation. Tribes having fewer sound elements in their language or dialect would dispense with the runes they did not require, while a tribe with a greater number of sound elements would invent new runes to cover them. Also some sounds would with time pass out of use, thus rendering the corresponding rune obsolete. This explains the variety of futharks and also suggests that no single futhark should be considered as 'more' correct than any other.

The nordic myths link the origin of runes with the discovery of speech, attributing both to Odin. He was, as the Romans understood him to be, the equivalent of their own Mercury, the god of knowledge and communication.

THE NORSE TAROT

The Norse Tarot has been designed to conform with the majority of traditional Tarot interpretations. The illustrations should convey recognizable meanings to the practised reader. Anyone first learning the Tarot with this deck will be able to apply their skills to other decks with ease.

In every case a presentation has been sought which conveys the meaning in both an original way and in a form compatable to the Nordic theme of the whole.

The Court cards, however (the King, Queen, etc.), have been changed slightly. The Page is now the Prince and the Knight has become the Princess. This eliminates certain difficulties that might arise when using Tarot Spreads which require a card chosen to represent the questioner.

The images of the Major Arcana may, in some instances, appear radically different to those of tranditional Tarot decks, but in all cases their interpretations remain the same.

CHAPTER 2

THE MAJOR ARCANA

The cards of the Tarot deck are divided into two parts. The first part is the Major Arcana consisting of 22 cards, and the second is the Minor Arcana with 56 cards.

The Major Arcana is the most important of the two. Numbered sequentially from 0 to 21, its cards represent the archetypal forces of nature. For purposes of divination they may be interpreted individually, but as a whole they convey a story of spiritual unfolding. They provide a detailed symbolic account of a progression from innocence through wordly knowledge and achievement to spiritual rebirth.

The Norse Tarot uses the symbolism of the Northern peoples, taking as its theme the central subject of their mythology. The first card, the Fool, shows Balder, the pure god of the sun. The following cards picture other Northern gods and mythological events. These represent the various stages of Balder's development and important turning points in his life.

Each card of the Major Arcana is also assigned a rune character. This provides further depth to their interpretation. The meanings of the runes are more general in nature than the cards and so must be read within the context of the neighbouring cards, and for this reason 'reversed' interpretations (for upside-down cards) are not given for the runes.

THE FOOL

INTERPRETATION
New beginnings; the start of a new cycle of activity; innocence and naïvety; a creative dreamer; hidden talents; optimism unaffected by past events; purity of purpose; impulsive thoughts and actions; unconventional ways of looking at things; the unexpected or unplanned may be about to happen.

REVERSED MEANING
Problems arising from recklessness or ill-considered decisions; immature or irrational actions; a poor application of energies.

THE RUNE
Sigel, the rune of the glittering sun. Signifying the life force; warmth; health and harmony.

BALDER

The child of Odin and Frigga, Balder the beautiful was the god of light, the god of the sun, purity and innocence. He was renowned for his radiance and good looks; anyone who set eyes upon him or chanced to hear him speak could not fail to love him, so harmonious was his presence. His brow was white and pure, his face so bright that shafts of sunlight appeared to shine all around him.

Because of her love for him, his mother Frigga went out and begged all of creation to swear never to do harm to Balder. She spoke to the birds that flew, the animals that walked, and the creatures that crawled, the flowers and forests, rocks and stones. All that she asked were happy to do her bidding, such was their love of Balder, and from that day forth he was invulnerable to all.

His home was the Hall of Breidablik, whose silver roof lay upon pillars of gold. It was a place of such purity that nothing unclean was ever allowed to enter. Here he lived with his wife Nanna (blossom), the daughter of Nip (bud), who like Balder was famed for her beauty and charm.

Balder is the god of the sun; he is pictured dressed in a white cloak and tunic representing his innocence, and symbolizing a white page upon which a story is about to be written. The morning sky is blue above him, and the full richness of the earth lies at his feet. The symbols of his solar origin are all around him — upon his brow he wears a golden disc, around his neck hangs a string of amber, on his right hand, on the finger of Apollo, he has a golden ring.

The border of his tunic is decorated with a design of alternating red and gold 'sigil' runes, the rune of the sun. His left hand is held palm upwards, showing that he is pure and unblemished, he has nothing to hide.

He runs for pleasure of running, for the joy of youth.

THE MAGICIAN

INTERPRETATION
Intelligence; knowledge; communication; planning; strength of will; organizing force; originality.

REVERSED MEANINGS
Trickery and cunning; devious manipulation; untrustworthiness; hesitation; inability to articulate one's thoughts; mental confusion.

THE RUNE
Peorth, meaning dice cup. Gambling; speculation; risks; placing oneself in the hands of another.

ODIN

Odin, the god of wisdom, was the highest of the Northern gods. He was the master of magic and god of war. His followers knew that if he wished, he could reward them well. But he was also considered to be a fickle god and was thought on occasions to turn against the faithful, giving victory in battle to the opposing side. For this reason one of his many names was the Trickster God.

From his throne on the mighty watchtower, Hlidskialf, he would look out over the whole world. Gazing over the lands of men, giants, dwarfs and elves, none could escape his all-seeing eye. He presided over the great hall of Gladsheim, which contained the 12 seats belonging to the council of the gods.

His second hall was Valhalla, the hall of the chosen dead. Here resided Odin's favourites, the Einheriar, the warriors who had fallen in battle. Together they would fight by day and, on being magically restored to health, would feast by night.

He possessed two ravens, Hugin (thought) and Munin (memory). They would fly off in the morning and spend the day searching the land; at nightfall they returned to whisper into his ears all they had seen and heard. He also kept two wolves as hunting dogs, named Geri and Freki.

The Trickster God, the god of wisdom, Odin stands with the four elemental weapons. The sword of air, the shield of earth, the chalice of water, and the wand of fire in the form of the magical spear, Gungnir, forged by the dwarfs. His cloak is blue, the colour of the sky, and his wide-brimmed hat hangs low, covering the empty socket of the sacrificed eye. His two ravens circle high above, and behind him stand the two wolves.

THE HIGH PRIESTESS

INTERPRETATION
Insight into problems produces a solution; hidden knowledge; change for the better; the favourable influence of a woman; intuition; secrets; psychic experiences.

REVERSED MEANING
Deception; confusion; uncertainty; lack of foresight; emotion; instability; a disruptive feminine influence.

THE RUNE
Ear, meaning sea or water and also earth or the grave. Cycles of change, times of transition, looking into or thinking of the future.

FRIGGA

The daughter of Fiorgyn and the sister of Jord, Frigga was considered to be the patroness of marriage, her health being toasted at the wedding feast. She was the goddess of the sky, and was represented in clothes the colour of the clouds. Sometimes she would be dressed brightly, in garments as white as snow and at other times more darkly, reflecting the ever-changing nature of the weather.

She had the ability to see into the future, but seldom revealed what she saw. Throughout the writings of the Northern peoples the power of prophecy was usually ascribed to women. Known by the name 'Volva', these women appear to have followed similar practices to the shamans of more recent times. They have been recorded as entering into a self-induced trance before being able to foretell the future.

In the card, Frigga is shown standing within a dark pool. This represents secrets of the unconciousness, the hidden mysteries which she guards and which she alone can share. She holds around herself a white gown, as if concealing her inner wisdom.

Taken together, the colours of her white gown and the cloak of deep red, edged in black, that hangs behind her over the throne, represent the three phases of the moon, and similarly the three ages of womanhood. Beyond the throne stand the twin stones that mark the entrance to her temple, these stand for the duality of opposites, and reflect the horns of the moon.

From her ears hang silver moons; low in the sky the moon itself can be seen.

THE EMPRESS

INTERPRETATION
A motherly figure; maternal care; fertility; growth;
abundance; domestic stability; happiness; pregnancy;
beauty.

REVERSED MEANING
Restriction by the control of a motherly figure; infertility;
unwanted pregnancy; female domination.

THE RUNE
Ger, meaning the fruitful part of the year, the harvest.
Abundance; reward for endeavours; fertility; marriage.

FREYA

Freya, the golden-haired, blue-eyed goddess of beauty, love and lovers. The wife of Odin, she was the twin sister of Frey and the daughter of Niord and Nerthus.

Besides being the goddess of beauty. Freya was also the leader of the Valkyrs, the choosers of the slain. Together they transported half of the dead heroes to her hall. This was Sessrymnir (the many seated), in the realms of Folksvang. Here the dead would be served by faithful wives and the women who had died before marriage.

She had many followers amongst women. Some were known to go with their husbands into battle, being killed as their men were killed, or to have thrown themselves upon their husbands' funeral pyres. They believed that if they died together, they would go side-by-side into Freya's joyful hall and be together forever.

Freya is the personification of the earth. She can both give and take away. She is fruitfulness and receptiveness. She could, when she so wished, take the shape of a bird. At other times she travelled in a chariot drawn by two cats. The cat and the swallow were two of the animals sacred to her.

She is pictured in the card wearing the gold and green colours of the harvest. Behind her the ears of wheat bend gently in the breeze. The swallows fly in the warming sunlight and the cat sits contentedly at her feet. Dressed in the accoutrements of the Valkyrs, she holds the shaft of a spear firmly in her hand.

THE EMPEROR

INTERPRETATION
A fatherly figure; paternal qualities; strength; the state; authority; power; practical knowledge; leadership; governments and controlling bodies; law; police.

REVERSED MEANING
Tyrannical oppression; mistrust of authority; lack of independence; breaking rules; misuse of force.

THE RUNE
Tir, meaning splendour, power and glory. Victory; success; prepared to fight for one's beliefs.

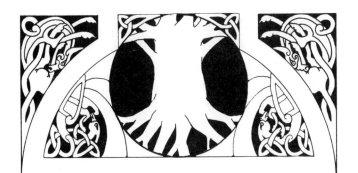

TYR

Tyr, the god of war and martial valour. According to some sources Tyr was the son of Odin; others say that the two were brothers. In earlier times he was the supreme sky god of the Northern peoples; however his position later declined in favour of Odin, and this may explain the conflicing accounts. Whatever the case, Tyr occupied one of the 12 thrones in the great council hall of the gods, Gladsheim.

His name was invokved by warriors, along with that of Odin, to give victory in battle. The sword was held sacred to him and sword dances were held in his honour. The rune associated with his name has been found scratched upon weapons to bring honour to the owner. Oaths were sworn upon sword blades. Once made they could only be broken upon penalty of the god's wrath.

He was a protector of the community, the giver of law and order. The Romans gave him the name Mars Thingus. This links together the aspects of the war god (Mars being the god of war) and the law giver; the Thing was the people's assembly at which disputes were settled and laws established. These two concepts are also linked in the Iclandic practice of solving an important legal dispute by means of a sword duel.

Tyr is shown seated upon his great throne of cold stone, robed in red, the symbolic colour of force and action. His face is stern, he is remote and severe — not a god to be trifled with.

THE HIGH PRIEST

INTERPRETATION
Spiritual advancement; teaching; good advice; conformity; orthodox views; conservative ideas; dogma; the Church; religious matters.

REVERSED MEANING
Indoctrination; mental and spiritual oppression; fanatical obsession; distorting the truth; propaganda; poor advice.

THE RUNE
Ing, meaning (according to the rune poem) the god who is carried in a wagon, i.e. Frey. Protection; fertility; abundance; safety.

FREY

The brother of Freya, Frey was of the race of Vanir; he was given by the Aesir, the realm of Alfheim (Fairyland), the home of the Light Elves.

His symbol was a golden boar, Hildisrin. Charms in the form of a boar were often worn by his followers. These have been found in many forms. There were the smaller images, worn as pendants or kept in a man's personal pouch. And larger more elaborate and often stylized decorations found on helmets and weapons of war. Unlike the charms of Tyr, which helped to achieve a desired end, the Charms of Frey were believed to protect the wearer from harm.

He was also the owner of the ship Skithblathnir. While being large enough to carry all the gods, it could be folded so small as to be easily held in the palm of the hand. The ship also had the ability to sail in any direction at Frey's will, as it always benefitted from a favourable wind.

The concept of the ship with Frey at its helm may be linked to a tradition once held in Sweden, where an image of Frey was carried in a special wagon. This took place in the autumn when the image was removed from his temple and ceremoniously transported from farmstead to farmstead. Throughout its travels the idol was believed to be invested with the presence of the god himself, to whom sacrifices would be made. In return his followers received his blessings. These would have included a promise of good fortune through the trials of winter and an assurance of prosperity in the year to come. In the vicinity of the wagon no sword could be drawn from its scabbard and no act of aggression perpetrated.

He raises his hand in blessing as his attendants carry him onwards in his ceremonial progress through the fields of autumn.

THE LOVERS

INTERPRETATION
A choice made from the heart not the mind; insight into partnerships; important decisions leading to new opportunities.

REVERSED MEANING
Indecision; inability to solve problems; contradictions; partnership dissolved as a result of external factors.

THE RUNE
Gyfu, meaning a gift. Generosity; love; an important development in an emotional relationship.

FREYA AND BRISINGAMAN

While travelling in Svartalfheim, the realm of the dark elves, Freya chanced to come across four brothers. They were dwarfs, the short misshaped people of the cavernous earth, busy in the forging of the wonderous necklace, Brisingaman. As her eyes fell upon the product of their dark skilled hands, she immediately fell in love with it and vowed that she should possess the necklace whatever the cost may be.

On completing their work the necklace is shown, as agreed, to the covertous Freya. With eyes stinging beneath the bright sun light, the eldest of the brother's offers it to her and makes their price known. Brisingaman is to be hers, a gift, if only she will spend a night with each of the four dwarfs. Now she must decide, should she remain faithful to Odin her husband or should she take the gift that she so desires?

Within the card, the dwarf holds the finished necklace for Freya to see. They are unobserved by Odin, but his messenger, the raven, looks on. Shall she allow her love of beautiful things and personal ornamentation override her loyalty to her husband, and her deep physical distaste of the dark elf and his brothers?

As she walks beneath the Northern sky, she has to choose. Odin or the gift?

THE CHARIOT

INTERPRETATION
Progress; success made through endeavour; firm control of
one's circumstances, self confidence; good health.

REVERSED MEANING
Loss of control; only partial or temporary success; lack of
organizational skills; imbalance; inability to adjust.

THE RUNE
Thorn, symbolizing the god Thor. Help or self help; self
protection and self preservation.

THOR

Thor, the god of thunder, was tall and strong. His hair was red. In moments of anger sparks would fly like lightening from his beard. Mjolnir was his hammer, Crusher its name. He hurled it at his enemies the Frost Giants, with great destructive power. However hard or far he threw it, it would return safely to his hand.

Thor was considered to be a benevolent deity and was worshipped widely throughout the Northern kingdoms. His popularity continued well into Christian times. Talismans in the shape of small hammers have been found along side crucifixes on sites of Viking and Anglo-Saxon occupation.

Thor lived in the hall of Bilskinir (Lightning), in the realm of Thrudvang, where the peasants were received after death. Thor was the god of the ordinary man, which probably explains his great popularity.

When the storm clouds gathered, the rumble and roar of thunder was thought to be the sound of the wheels of his chariot. Drawn by the two dark goats. Tanngniostr (tooth cracker) and Tanngrisnr (tooth gnasher), he traversed the heavens. Sparks would constantly fly from the teeth and hoofs of his goats.

JUSTICE

INTERPRETATION
Justice; balance; truth; judgement; legal matters; arbitration and agreement; harmony; documents to inspect or to sign; external influences.

REVERSED MEANING
An unsympathetic decision; adverse judgement; bias; bigotry; no hope of justice; fighting against the legal system.

THE RUNE
Lagu, meaning that which is laid or fixed, i.e. the law, unalterable; unchangable; beyond argument.

FORSETI

Forseti was the son of Balder, god of light, and Nanna, goddess of purity. With parents such as these Forsetti was considered to be the most gentle and the wisest of all the gods.

His home was Glitnir, where he held the position of arbiter and law giver to the gods. Sitting upon his throne each day he would settle their problems. With the utmost care he would consider every side, every aspect of the question in hand. Finally pronouncing a decision of such unequivicable soundness, all were happy to abide by his will.

His name was invoked by all who required help in legal matters, but his assistance would only be given to the just party. No one dared to break a vow made in his name for fear of raising his displeasure. His eloquent words never failed to persuade even the most bitter of enemies to reconcile their differences.

Here he is shown holding a great two edged fighting axe. His hand holds it balanced perfectly, preventing it falling to either side, symbolizing his impartiality.

Behind him, the design incorporates two equal parts suggesting the way in which a problem balances with its own solution. Combining together to form an inseparable whole, the answer must complement the question. The spirals indicate the complexity of the balance and the difficulty that may be met in unravelling arguments to reach the truth.

THE HERMIT

INTERPRETATION
Warnings and advice; a need for caution; withdrawal; isolation; foresight; guidance; wisdom.

REVERSED MEANING
Unheeded advice; ignored warnings; introversion; hiding; assistance refused; false information.

THE RUNE
Eolh, meaning protection. A defensive position; a place of shelter; a guardian or patron.

HEIMDALL

Heimdall was the guardian of the gods. He watched unceasingly over Bifrost, the Rainbow Bridge that linked the earth with the realm of the gods.

He had senses so keen that he could hear the sound of the grass growing on the hillsides and the sound of wool upon a sheep's back. He was able to see things clearly at a distance of a hundred miles, by day and night. Because of this he was considered a god of great intelligence having knowledge of all things. Also he required very little sleep and was able to keep up his vigilance almost without interruption.

To help him further in his task the gods gave him two wonderful gifts. The first was a fine sword and the second, the trumpet Giallarhorn, upon which he was to sound a warning if ever the enemies of the gods ventured to approach their home, Asgard.

He was always depicted dressed in white and was known as Heimdall the Bright, he was the personification of benevolent fire. The rainbow bridge was formed of three colours, the red of fire, the blue of air and the green of deep sea.

In the card Heimdall looks out over the rainbow bridge with his horn in his hand and sword ready by his side. He is clothed in white, but his cloak is checked in red, symbolizing the power of controlled fire. His arm is raised in a salute to the dawn, and beneath him in the morning light lie the cold stones and snow of his lonely mountain top vantage point.

THE WHEEL OF FORTUNE

INTERPRETATION
Change for the better; motion; improvement; good fortune and prosperity; starting a new cycle of events; the unfolding future looks good.

REVERSED MEANING
A turn for the worse; bad luck; the past catches up; an inability or unwillingness to adapt to change.

THE RUNE
Rad, meaning travel or riding. Movement; change, travel; continuity.

THE NORNS

The three Norns were believed to govern the fate of man. Even the gods were subject to their decrees. They could neither question their judgement nor influence their will. The Norns were three sisters, whose names were Urd, Verdandi and Skuld. They were respectively the personifications of the past, the present, and the future.

Symbolzing the concept of time, they were each represented as being of a different physical age. Urd was very old and continually stared back into the past. Verdandi was mature and active seeing only the present, while Skuld, the youngest of the three, always looked far ahead in the opposite direction to her elder sister Urd. She was also represented as being veiled to indicate the uncertainty and hidden nature of the future.

Together they wove the web of fate, from whose strings none could escape. Urd and Verdandi, the past and present, were considered to be benign and helpful spinning their web with the utmost care, while Skuld (future) was thought to be constantly undoing their good work.

In the card they are shown beneath the tree Ygdrasil, in their traditional positions. Urd looks to the past, the young Skuld looks in the opposite direction, while between them Verdandi has her eyes set firmly upon the present. Before them is the pool of the Urdar fountain, with which they water the roots of the sacred tree. Upon the pool lived two swans. From them all the birds of the earth were said to be descended. It was also believed that at times the Norns themselves would visit the world in the shape of swans.

STRENGTH

INTERPRETATION
Control of passions and emotions; suppression of undesirable thoughts and actions; self-discipline; courage; strength in overcoming difficulties; control over ones' environment and way of life.

REVERSED MEANING
Uncontrolled emotion; unbridled lust and perversions; self-indulgence; temperamental; weakness of mind or body.

THE RUNE
Ur, meaning wild ox or trials of strength. Achievement; success in examinations; maturity; proving ones self; determination.

THE BINDING OF FENRIS

Secretly in Jotunheim, Loki married the giantess Angurboda. Some time later she bore him three monstrous children. One was Hel, who was to become the goddess of the Underworld. Another was Iormungandr, the Great Serpent. The wolf Fenris was the third. For a time the existance of the three was kept from the gods. But before very long, they had grown to such an extent, they could no longer be concealed within the cave of their birth.

From his throne Hlidskiaf, the all seeing Odin became aware of their presence upon the earth. Soon he grew alarmed at the rate at which their size increased. Seeing that the monsters might pose a threat to the peace of Asgard, he determined to dispose of them.

Hel he cast into the depths of Niflheim, giving her the land of the dead for her abode, and Iormungandr was flung far into the sea. But Fenris he kept, thinking that with the proper kindness and understanding, the wolf might be trained to serve the gods. To Odin's dismay however, Fenris daily increased in size, strength and ferociousness. Eventually the god realized the impossibility of his task.

After consulting the other gods, it was agreed that to kill the creature would violate the laws of Asgard; the only path left open was to make him secure and unable to do harm.

After several failures the gods armed themselves with a silken rope, magically fashioned by the dark elves of Svartalfheim. The gods explained to Fenris that they wished to test his enormous strength against that of the rope. But Fenris, being suspicious, would only agree if one of the gods would consent to place a hand between his jaws. So finally Tyr agreed and he bound the wolf with the magical rope. Fenris, in anger at finding himself unable to struggle free, bit Tyr's hand off at the wrist.

THE HANGED MAN

INTERPRETATION
Voluntary sacrifice for a belief or an ideal; giving to receive; exchanging material comforts for spiritual advancement.

REVERSED MEANING
Punishment; pain; loss; selfishness; placing too much emphasis upon material things; fear of progress.

THE RUNE
Os, meaning god but usually considered to refer to Odin ('Os is the origin of all speech' says the Old English Rune Poem). Knowledge; wisdom; communication.

ODIN'S SACRIFICE

Odin hung upon the branches of the sacred Tree. For nine days and nine nights he suffered. Self wounded by his spear, sacrificed by his hand, an offering unto himself.

In agony and torment he stared into the bottomless depths of Niflheim, searching the dark pool in silence. Finally, with great effort, he reached down before him. His hand was chilled to the bone in the ice cold waters. With a cry of triumph he grasped the knowledge he sought — the Sacred Runes, their magic and their power.

He took the Runes and he used them well. He carved them upon the shaft of his spear; he carved runes upon all things. By this means he obtained power over all.

DEATH

INTERPRETATION
Casting off the past; looking to the future; transformation; a turning point; change of personality; complete change in ones way of life or circumstances; a new view of the future.

REVERSED MEANING
Forces or unpleasant change; a difficult transition; depression; loss of hope; despondancy; prolonged upheavals.

THE RUNE
Yr, translated as yew tree, the tree associated with death. Resurrection; a small disaster; hindrance.

THE DEATH OF BALDER

Upon the plain of Ida was the playground of the gods, Idavold. Here the gods amused themselves by casting all manner of weapons at Balder. As Frigga had extracted an oath from all things to do Balder no harm, he was safe from their missiles.

Loki however discovered that Frigga had, while engaged in taking the oaths, considered the mistletoe too immature for such an important undertaking and so passed it by. Immediately he went to an oak that stood by the gate to Valhalla and found mistletoe growing. By means of his magic he fashioned the plant into a spear.

Returning to Idavold, Loki gave the spear to the blind god Hodur, suggesting that he joined the sport and cast it at Balder. So Hodur, with his hand guided by Loki, threw the shaft. Balder fell dead; his bright flesh pierced by the spear.

The gods grieved bitterly as they carried his body away. All this had been fortold. His death would herald many changes, but what the future held in store they knew not.

TEMPERANCE

INTERPRETATION
Optimism; a way out of difficulties; opposition transformed into harmony; co-operation; a truce; the agreement of opposites; reconciliation; balance.

REVERSED MEANINGS
Advantages lost by mishandling the situation; disunity; failure to agree or adapt; leads to loss.

THE RUNE
Beorc, signifying spring or rebirth. The celebration of a fortunate event; a new life.

HERMOD'S RIDE

Balder was dead, and his spirit passed on to the other world. Frigga and Odin promised great rewards to anyone who would help return their son to the living. They asked for someone to go down into the depths of Niflheim and persuade Hel to release her beautiful prize. Because of his love for Balder, Hermod agreed that he should go.

To assist him in his quest Odin gave his horse Seipnir, whose hoofs would be sure of foot on the dark and slippery descent into Hel's kingdom. Riding down, and ever down into the very depths of the earth, past the Hel hound Garm, and on through Hel's gate, he at last came before the pale presence of Loki's daughter.

He implored her, he begged her, on the behalf of all the gods of Asgard, to release their beloved companion. In silence she heard his words and in silence she sat, giving his plea much consideration. Finally she spoke, declaring her promise. If the whole earth shed tears for Balder then he would be free to rejoin the living.

Hermod was heartened by her words for he knew that none upon the earth, or within it, wished the bright Balder any harm. All would be willing to help secure his release, so great was their love for him. With her words in his ears and joy in his heart, he turned his horse to carry the news back to the grieving gods of Asgard.

THE DEVIL

INTERPRETATION
Bound by one's physical desires; temptation towards evil; a slave to materialism; selfishness; a need to supress one's animal instincts and to control harmful tendencies.

REVERSED MEANING
Held back by a self-created block; self-destructive behaviour; misuse of power or position; release from bondage.

THE RUNE
Nyd, meaning need, necessity or thralldom. Affliction; subjugation; endurance; patience; a time for caution.

THE PUNISHMENT OF LOKI

On hearing Hermod's tidings of the promise of Hel to release
Balder, the gods were overjoyed. Immediately they sent out
messengers. Far and wide, in every direction they rode. All
they met were eager to help, all were happy to shed tears
for the god they loved. All but one. Deep within a cave a
giantess vowed that she would never weep for Balder's sake.

The gods were downcast, their sorrow was great. They
asked who was this giantess that she should hate Balder so.
Eventually they discovered to their dismay, that the giantess
was Loki in disguise. They searched afar to seek wherever
he might hide, and when at last they found him, they took
him and beneath the earth they bound him.

Skaldi the giantess fastened a serpent above his head, its
ice cold venom dripping down upon his upturned face. But
his faithful wife Sigyn sat by his side catching the falling
drops until the end of time. Whenever she went to empty
her dish, it was said, the earth would quake as he writhed
in torment.

THE TOWER

INTERPRETATION
Sudden changes; conflict; destruction; unexpected setback; sudden realization or unexpected insight; release from tension; end of the old system, the beginning of the new.

REVERSED MEANING
Unnecessary suffering; a disaster that may have been avoided; a lack of self-preservation.

THE RUNE
Hagall, meaning hail, disruption; oppression; constraint; loss of control over one's personal situation.

RAGNAROK

Beneath the earth the dragon Nidhug knawed at the roots of the World Ash. The seas were swept into a fury by the writhings of the Midgard Snake. Upon the waves rode the ship Nagilfar, formed entirely from the nail parings of the dead. At its helm was Loki, newly released from his bonds. A second ship came sailing through the Northern fog, Hrymard, and the Frost Giants bore down upon Asgard.

The three birds of doom cried out their warning. Heimdall blew upon his horn, the long feared blast echoing through the mountains. Hel rose from her confines and with her came the dragon who flew over the battle plain bearing the dead upon its wings. On landing his ship Loki, at the head of his terrible host, marched onwards leading his legions towards the final battle.

Surt and his sons crossed Bifrost. Beneath their pounding feet the arch cracked, and in splinters of light it came falling from the sky. The gods knew their end was near and gathering their forces they rode to meet their foe. Beneath the rumbling Ash, the Norns sat, their faces covered, their web in tatters lying at their feet.

The battle was fought upon Vigridi plain, the two sides at last meeting. Odin was amongst the first to fall, engulfed within the flaming jaws of Fenris. Frey too fell, beneath Surt's cruel sword. Heimdall slew Loki but could not rise from his own wounds. Tyr died in the act of slaying Garm. Thor, with a powerful stroke from Mjolnir smashed the skull of the Midgard Snake, but drowned in the venomous flow that came issuing forth from the dead monster's jaws.

All the gods, the Einheriar and their enemies fell. Flames consumed the Tree. The earth burned and the oceans boiled, the seas rose and flooded the land. The heavens filled with blackened smoke. The battle was over and chaos reigned.

All, both good and evil, had perished.

THE STAR

INTERPRETATION
Hope; clear thoughts; new confidence; the light at the end of the tunnel; optimism; the calm after the storm; a promise of a brighter future.

REVERSED MEANING
False hopes; self-deception; incapable of positive thinking; a lack of trust in others; blind to surrounding change; pessimism.

THE RUNE
Cen, meaning torch. A comforting hand; positive thoughts; recovery; new relationships.

THE STAR OF HOPE

Beneath the blackened sky the earth lay submerged. Slowly the dark waters subsided. The world was calm and still, its face barren.

But within its depths two are sleeping. Lif and Liflhrasir, man and wife, secure from the troubles in their refuge, waiting for a time when once again they will be able to walk safely upon the face of the earth.

Now the sky clears and a solitary star begins to shine, weakly at first then growing stronger. One by one, other stars take their places. They return to their former positions, unseen by the eyes of sleeping man.

THE MOON

INTERPRETATION
A time for reassessment; introspection; imagination; dreams; psychic happenings; intuition succeeds where reason might fail.

REVERSED MEANING
Illusion; fantasy; escapism; disguised actions; hidden worries, unseen dangers; daydreams replace reality.

THE RUNE
Is, meaning ice or winter. A period of dormancy; little action; delay; rest.

MANI'S SON

A new moon rises from the depths. Casting off the cloak of darkness he reveals his pale face to the world.

His father, Mani, was devoured by the wolf Hati before the fall of the gods. Now he stands in his father's place. Beneath him the oceans begin to sway, tides fall upon the shore, and on the earth dark shadows hide secrets and rumours of imagined movement.

THE SUN

INTERPRETATION
Material happiness; great joy; good fortune; success; achievement; recovery; good health; rewards; clear perspectives.

REVERSED MEANING
Joy tinged with sadness; unsatisfactory achievements; unrewarding success; happiness of a transient nature.

THE RUNE
Winn, meaning joy. Happiness; health; energy; the enjoyment of a secure and stable position.

THE DAUGHTER OF SOL

The sun, the bright daughter of Sol, outshines her mother as she reveals her glory to the earth below. The Sun's beneficial rays pour down, giving warmth to the earth and within the ground life begins to stir. Flowers rise and show their rich colours; the trees laden with fruit reach up towards the sky.

Lif and his wife Liflhrasir climb from their resting place. Rejoicing they walk upon a green earth cleansed of all suffering and evil.

JUDGEMENT

INTERPRETATION
Spiritual awakening; new doors are opening; a time for positive action; a change for the better; renewed energy; decisions leading to improvement.

REVERSED MEANING
Wasted opportunities; indecision leading to delay; fear of the unkown; postponement of results.

THE RUNE
Ethel, symbolizing inheritance and homeland. Legacy; returning home; hereditary possession of land; continuation; succession.

THE NEW GODS

The old gods are gone forever, remaining only in memory. Their sons now take their place — upon the plain of Ida they meet.

First come Vali and Vidar, the brave sons of Odin. Then, bearing their fathers sacred hammer, come the children of Thor, Modi and Magni. They are met by Hodur and the blind Honir, and together on Idavold they joyously exchange greetings. From there they will retire to the hall of Gimli, its roof glittering gold beneath the glowing sun, and their faces bright with joy, to await the coming of their lord.

THE WORLD

INTERPRETATION
Completion; the achievement of objectives; harmony; fulfilment; moving on; the end of an era.

REVERSED MEANING
Nothing more is to be done; no further progress is possible; stagnation; a loss of momentum.

THE RUNE
Mann, meaning man, mankind or humanity. Unification; homogeny; coming together; becoming one.

BALDER REBORN

Hel has gone, the underworld is no more, and Balder, bright as the rising sun, returns.

Now there are new gods in heaven and he comes to lead them, to rule over the new people on the earth below. The dark past is forgotten; his eyes look to a glorious future.

The card shows Balder reborn. Gone are his earthly weapons, his sword, dagger and spear. He needs them no more. His purity is transformed, raised to a higher plane. He is haloed in golden light symbolizing his great sanctity.

CHAPTER 3

THE MINOR ARCANA

The Minor or Lesser Arcana is divided into four suits of 14 cards each. These Tarot suits correspond to the four suits found in a standard pack of playing cards. However in place of the three Court cards found in a pack of playing cards (King, Queen and Jack), the Tarot has four. In the Norse Tarot these are King, Queen, Princess and Prince. The remaining cards in each suit are numbered from one to ten, and their interpretations are conveyed by the illustrations they bear.

Each suit represents one of the four elements, fire, water, air and earth, and also the astrological signs associated with each element. The symbolism of the elements appears prominently in the Court cards. Flames are shown on those of the suit of Wands, water on those of Cups. The people illustrated on these cards are dressed in colours corresponding to their element; the Wands of fire are clothed in red, the Discs of earth in green or brown, and so forth.

On a more mundane level, each suit represents an aspect of daily life.

Suit	Element	Aspect	Astrological signs
Wands	Fire	Action	Aries, Leo, Sagittarius
Cups	Water	Emotions	Cancer, Scorpio, Pisces
Swords	Air	Mind	Gemini, Libra, Aquarius
Discs	Earth	Money	Taurus, Virgo, Capricorn

SIGNIFICATORS

The Court cards are also used as Significators — a card chosen for some spreads to represent the questioner. The reader may choose the Significator in two ways. If the questioner is well known to the reader a card is chosen that most reflects the questioner's personality. Otherwise choose a card which corresponds to the questioner's birth sign.

The Kings and the Princes represent mature adults and young males respectively. Similarly the Queens and the Princesses represent females. In general an adult is assumed to be someone above the age of 20, but obviously the reader should use his or her own judgement to decide precisely where to draw the line. For example, a woman aged about 40 and born under the sign of Libra, the Significator would be Queen of Swords.

ACE OF WANDS

THE CARD
A ceremonial sceptre symbolizing the element of fire. It significes the flame of the thunderbolt. The illustration shows the decorated whetstone sceptre found during the excavation of the Sutton Hoo ship burial.

INTERPRETATION
New beginnings, whether the birth of a child, an idea, or an enterprise; inspiration, invention and creation.

REVERSED MEANING
Failure to take advantage of ideas; a decline; destructiveness; impotence.

TWO OF WANDS

THE CARD
An explorer has travelled as far as the land beneath his feet
will allow. Now, standing by the sea's edge, he longs to move
onward to further new discoveries.

INTERPRETATION
Enterprise; success gained through hard work, but
overshadowed by the urge to move on to futher triumphs.

REVERSED MEANING
Success through underhand means; energy put to wrong
aims.

THREE OF WANDS

THE CARD
Two merchants walk from their ships discussing a successful trading venture.

INTERPRETATION
Strength and success resulting from a good partnership; looking forward to a promising future.

REVERSED MEANING
Failure to accept help through pride; the over estimation of own strength; disappointment after a good start.

FOUR OF WANDS

THE CARD
Now the builder has finished his work he rests for a while
between the roof supports of his new home.

INTERPRETATION
Completion of work and celebration; a period of well earned
rest; satisfaction.

REVERSED MEANING
Premature or undeserved celebration; obstacles and delays
soon passing; poor workmanship.

FIVE OF WANDS

THE CARD
Five warriors locked in combat. Whether real or in practice, each is doing his utmost to win.

INTERPRETATION
Competition and opposition; a struggle to succeed; unrelenting effort is necessary.

REVERSED MEANING
Misplaced competitiveness or aggression.

SIX OF WANDS

THE CARD
The Viking warrior stands at the prow of his ship surrounded by his followers. They are returning victorious from their adventures at sea. A shield divided into six segments, representing the sun and its fire aspect, hangs over the side of the ship.

INTERPRETATION
A triumph or victory for the questioner; good news is on its way; problems will be overcome.

REVERSED MEANING
Delay; a battle to come in which the opposition may win; treachery and disloyalty.

SEVEN OF WANDS

THE CARD
The warrior stands alone against his adversaries. Only his continued courage and strength saves him from being overwhelmed.

INTERPRETATION
Powerful opposition, seemingly insurmountable; fighting against the odds, but victory is possible through unrelenting hard work.

REVERSED MEANING
Inability to continue, even when victory is in sight; danger from overwork.

EIGHT OF WANDS

THE CARD
A small vessel travels in haste towards the shore carrying the seafarers home. The men row hard with the promise of a speedy landfall.

INTERPRETATION
Sudden movement or release; a short period of high activity; news; messages; a homecoming.

REVERSED MEANING
Bad or disappointing news; misplaced effort, ill-judged actions; delays or a cancellation.

NINE OF WANDS

THE CARD
The warrior awaits his enemy safe in the knowledge that he has the full backing of his family behind him. His position is secure.

INTERPRETATION
A secure position with considerable resources to fall back upon; support and help in a time of conflict.

REVERSED MEANING
The loss of a secure position; exceeding one's abilities; obstacles; downfall.

TEN OF WANDS

THE CARD
A richly-dressed merchant burdens himself with the menial task of carrying his wares. He should leave the job to his workers and occupy himself with affairs befitting his rank.

INTERPRETATION
The difficulties of success; the burden of worry; the inability to disseminate responsibility amongst others; overwork.

REVERSED MEANING
Energies being misused; oppression of subordinates.

PRINCE OF WANDS

THE CARD
In the cold of the Northern night the Prince warms himself
before the fire, spear in hand and ever vigilant.

INTERPRETATION
An enthusiastic and resourceful person — the bearer of
news; intelligent and reliable.

REVERSED MEANING
An untrustworthy youth — vengeful and deceitful; the
bringer of bad news.

PRINCESS OF WANDS

THE CARD
The Princess holds aloft a burning torch to light the way
to the exit of the cave.

INTERPRETATION
An impulsive, restless person, possibly an extrovert; perhaps
a sudden separation or departure.

REVERSED MEANING
A quarrelsome person, narrow-minded and unreasoning.

QUEEN OF WANDS

THE CARD
The Queen stands in a burnt field, but from the ashes will grow next years golden harvest.

INTERPRETATION
A strong but protective woman; generous and kind; sensible and intelligent.

REVERSED MEANING
Bad tempered; domineering; jealous and deceitful.

KING OF WANDS

THE CARD
Beneath the summer sky stands the King. His fiery cloak is caught upon the wind but he is unmoving, his feet fixed firmly upon the ground.

INTERPRETATION
Strong-minded, honest, positive and optimistic; a born leader; fatherly.

REVERSED MEANING
Good natured and tolerant, but superficial, theatrical and dogmatic.

ACE OF CUPS

THE CARD
A richly worked silver chalice, decorated with gold panels and bosses of coloured enamel.

INTERPRETATION
Joy and contentment; the beginning of a relationship or friendship; possibly a wedding, leading to a happy marriage; a gift or a birth.

REVERSED MEANING
Repressed emotion; barrenness; a poor choice of marriage partner; self interest.

TWO OF CUPS

THE CARD
The card shows two young people together in their home, sharing a drink. The man holds the woman's shoulder showing his affection for her, while she gazes upwards into his eyes. Around them are all the possessions of the home. They have stability and are happy together.

INTERPRETATION
Partnerships on all levels — friendship, romance, business; may also indicate two people coming together again after an argument.

REVERSED MEANING
A parting, either temporary or for good; desired partnerships may not be as good as hoped for.

THREE OF CUPS

THE CARD
A happy scene as the birth of a child is celebrated by the infant's mother, father and grandfather.

INTERPRETATION
A celebration or joyous occasion; good news; a reunion; success; favourable completion of a project; great happiness.

REVERSED MEANING
Over indulgence; concealing or ignoring a disappointment or disaster; intoxication; drowning one's sorrows; ignorant or blind to reality.

FOUR OF CUPS

THE CARD
A young woman sits alone on the sand by the sea. The sky is blue, she has all that she could wish for, but she is unhappy and dissatisfied with her life. She sees herself in the position of the goblet she holds, empty and without hope, while she overlooks the three other goblets full of promise and possibilities.

INTERPRETATION
Indecision and dissatisfaction with one's position; an inability to see the advantages that are available; boredom with life.

REVERSED MEANING
Make the most of the opportunities that present themselves; novelty; new experiences.

FIVE OF CUPS

THE CARD
A youth grasps one chalice firmly in his hand while looking at those lost in the sea beyond his reach.

INTERPRETATION
Despite losses one should not forget what remains; crying over spilt milk does no good — look to the future not the past; useless worry.

REVERSED MEANING
Unexpected anxieties and unforseen problems; unwanted changes in way of life.

SIX OF CUPS

THE CARD
The man and wife remember their own childhood as they proudly watch their two young children playing together contentedly.

INTERPRETATION
Links with the past; happy memories of youth; taking advantage of previous good luck or achievements; satisfaction; meeting an old friend.

REVERSED MEANING
Living in or longing for the past; resistance or an inability to adapt to change; remembering the good things of the past and ignoring the bad, self-deluded nostalgia.

SEVEN OF CUPS

THE CARD
The man wakes in the night to be confronted by three dwarfs bearing gifts. Is he dreaming or are they real? The seven golden chalices of promise may be illusory but they could be real — he cannot tell.

INTERPRETATION
A card of confusion. Unreal or unreliable advantages; nothing suggested is permanent or to be trusted at face value.

REVERSED MEANING
The desire, willpower or determination is present to sort muddled things out; alternatively, a person living in a fantasy world, totally divorced from reality.

EIGHT OF CUPS

THE CARD
Someone setting out on a journey, leaving the home and valuables behind. The door is left open for anyone to take whatever they will. The traveller does not intend to return.

INTERPRETATION
A change in beliefs or affections; setting out in a search for new and better things; the rejection of present stability or success to answer a need for something more worth while; a disagreement between physical and spiritual needs.

REVERSED MEANING
The search for an impossible ideal leads to the rejection of an advantageous position; restlessness; ill-considered change.

NINE OF CUPS

THE CARD
A happy man. He is content with the material aspects of
life and waits for friends to join him and share his hospitality.

INTERPRETATION
Satisfaction with one's achievements in life; contentment;
generous and sociable; continued happiness in the future.

REVERSED MEANING
Self-satisfied and self-indulgent; complacent; reluctant to
see the faults of others; over generosity or, conversely, a
complete lack of generosity; selfishness.

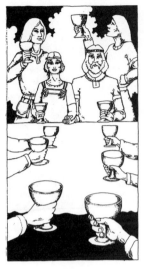

TEN OF CUPS

THE CARD
The couple celebrate their happiness with their family and friends, who join in a toast to their good health and prosperity. All are happy and joyful.

INTERPRETATION
Happiness and success; a peaceful and secure environment; lasting contentment.

REVERSED MEANING
Less permanent joy; changes in routine; disruption, possibly caused by new aquaintances or young people; antisocial behaviour; loss of friendship.

PRINCE OF CUPS

THE CARD
The young Prince stands before a dark mountain pool, into which flows the water of a bright stream. He holds out his chalice as if offering it to someone unseen.

INTERPRETATION
An artistic person; he is fond of quiet reflection and meditation but may tend to be a dreamer and romantic at times; he is knowledgable and gives advice freely.

REVERSED MEANING
An impractical person, who is all thought and no action; selfish, secretive and unhelpful; appreciates art but is unable to create anything of beauty himself.

PRINCESS OF CUPS

THE CARD
The Princess stands by the side of the lake, the mountains high above the pines in the background. She looks deeply into her carefully held chalice.

INTERPRETATION
An intelligent person; the bringer of ideas and the provider of opportunities; she needs constant intellectual stimulus in order to retain interest and can be easily distracted.

REVISED MEANING
An unreliable person, idle and fraudulant; unable to differentiate between truth and falsehood.

QUEEN OF CUPS

THE CARD
The Queen stands upon a rock before a wide river that runs unceasingly from the distant snow-capped mountains. She looks around with an air of knowingness about her.

INTERPRETATION
She relies upon her intuition which can be trusted in preference to common sense, but is easily influenced by others; imaginative and affectionate.

REVERSED MEANING
A dreamer, untrustworthy and unreliable; her opinions and loyalties change unpredictably without reason.

KING OF CUPS

THE CARD
With his cloak blowing in the wind, the King holds a chalice high in offering to the sea.

INTERPRETATION
A gifted negotiator; a manipulator; a diplomat; a leader who shuns the limelight; helpful and considerate. As he prefers to work behind the scenes, his aims are sometimes mistrusted, but he is always respected.

REVERSED MEANING
Seeking self-advancement. He is treacherous and dishonest; unscrupulous, with no moral concerns.

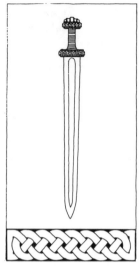

ACE OF SWORDS

THE CARD
A stong bladed sword of the type used by the warriors of Northern and Western europe during the period of Viking activity.

INTERPRETATION
A new start or plan; new ideas; triumph of intellect; change of ideas; progress.

REVERSED MEANING
Destruction; excessive or misused force; insanity or mental illness.

TWO OF SWORDS

THE CARD
Two opposing warrior chiefs put aside their swords and disagreements to join together in a game of chess. The game may be played for enjoyment or it may be to settle their differences without resorting to arms.

INTERPRETATION
Differences resolved; peace restored; equilibrium; balance; friendship rising from conflict.

REVERSED MEANING
Unstable or insecure balance; tension; lack of trust between friends; a threat of hostility.

THREE OF SWORDS

THE CARD
A battle is to be fought and the men are called to arms. The head of the family and his sons take up their swords and prepare to leave, but his wife fears that her youngest son is too young to fight and she begs him not to go.

INTERPRETATION
Separation and heart break; disruption; strife; upheavals in the home; loss, or fear of loss.

REVERSED MEANING
War and sorrow; conflict and quarrels; discord.

FOUR OF SWORDS

THE CARD
The man rests in his bed. He is recovering from wounds received in a recent battle. Soon he will be well again and he looks forward to renewed activity.

INTERPRETATION
Recovery; rest after strife; an opportunity for recuperation during a conflict; temporary relief from anxiety.

REVERSED MEANING
A long illness; forced isolation; possible imprisonment or hospitalization; failure of peace negotiations; depression.

FIVE OF SWORDS

THE CARD
In the background people helplessly watch their homes and possessions burning. As the smoke rises in the air, their oppressors move onwards.

INTERPRETATION
Defeat; triumph for enemies; loss of possessions; failure must be accepted before new advances may be made.

REVERSED MEANING
Failure through indecision or treachery; confusion; insanity; jealousy and revenge; paranoia.

SIX OF SWORDS

THE CARD
A woman aided by a cloaked man boards a ship preparing to sail. Upon the quay five swordsmen look down.

INTERPRETATION
Leaving troubles behind; solving problems by use of the intellect; long journeys; flight from danger.

REVERSED MEANING
Temporary success, running away from problems; escapism; insufficient effort used in dealing with difficulties; new problems lie ahead.

SEVEN OF SWORDS

THE CARD
Within the dragons lair the man moves with stealth. He has found what he seeks and now he must make good his escape before the dragon wakes.

INTERPRETATION
A need for care or cunning; courage is required but a head-on attack would be disastrous; diplomacy.

REVERSED MEANING
Foolhardy action; dangerous risks taken with no purpose or advantage in mind; failure to complete actions.

EIGHT OF SWORDS

THE CARD
A weaponless man is surrounded by eight hostile men armed with swords.

INTERPRETATION
Major difficulties; restriction; powerless to change one's position; wait awhile before attempting anything.

REVERSED MEANING
Release from an apparently inescapable position; restrictions will soon be lifted; hard work with no reward.

NINE OF SWORDS

THE CARD
The woman weeps, her tears fall upon the cold earth. The swords stand like grave markers — one lies broken on the ground. She has lost all she ever had.

INTERPRETATION
Despair; depression; disappointment; failure; violence; cruelty; scandal; self-destruction; martyrdom; suffering.

REVERSED MEANING
Isolation; agony; no help in sight; cut off from assistance; suicidal actions; total loss.

TEN OF SWORDS

THE CARD
A warrior threatened by opposition gathers all the weapons he can find and prepares to do battle.

INTERPRETATION
Loss of perspective; overreacting to problems; confusion, possibly insanity; failure; misfortune; ruin.

REVERSED MEANING
Momentary or illusory advantage; suffering will continue; insanity; grief.

PRINCE OF SWORDS

THE CARD
The Prince stands with his feet firmly on the ground, resting his hands upon his sword.

INTERPRETATION
A watchful person; a good observer; a skilled negotiator; a diplomat; able to see to the root of a problem.

REVERSED MEANING
Devious and underhand; prying into the affairs of others; two-faced; a spy.

PRINCESS OF SWORDS

THE CARD
The Princess stands upon the mountain top. The air is clear and fresh around her. She holds her sword with grace and balance.

INTERPRETATION
An active and highly-skilled person; someone who works well under pressure; a warrior who believes that attack is the best form of defence.

REVERSED MEANING
A dishonest and tricky opponant; violent and headstrong; a tendency to leave things uncompleted.

QUEEN OF SWORDS

THE CARD
The Queen stands in a field of wheat. The grasses blow gently in the breeze and she holds her sword casually with both hands.

INTERPRETATION
An intelligent and highly perceptive woman; decisive; penetrating; versatile; uses her skills to her own advantage.

REVERSED MEANING
Intolerant; unreliable; devious; good at disguising the truth; a gossip.

KING OF SWORDS

THE CARD
Sitting upon a rock with his cloak wrapped about him, the King looks into the distance. His mind is on many things, yet he is ready for action at a moment's notice.

INTERPRETATION
A man ruled by his intellect rather than his emotions; a lover of rules and authority; always looking ahead; favours new ideas to tradition.

REVERSED MEANING
Calculating; impersonal; unfeeling; indecisive; may be overcome with fanatical zeal.

ACE OF DISCS

THE CARD
A disc of interlacing birds and animals. There are 12 dog-like creatures in four groups of three, chasing their own tails. The dogs represent the 12 months of the year, the four groups are the four seasons. The eight birds represent the eight worlds that surround Middle Earth — the world of man.

INTERPRETATION
Contentment, happiness and news; perhaps the coming of wealth and prosperity; a new job or business proposition.

REVERSED MEANING
The negative side of wealth — materialism overrides all else; obsessive greed; clinging to the past; fear of death or of change.

TWO OF DISCS

THE CARD
The woman provides a meal for her father and her son. The child's grandfather gives him a model of his father's ship and explains how one day he too shall sail the seas, as all the men in his family have done for generations before him.

INTERPRETATION
Change combined with stability; natural fluctuations in fortune; balance and continuity; the passing on of responsibility.

REVERSED MEANING
A reluctance to change; lack of balance; no foresight; living for today with no thought for tomorrow.

THREE OF DISCS

THE CARD
Three coins fall from the merchant's purse onto the hand of the craftsman. In the background are the shops selling their wares.

INTERPRETATION
A business venture; a combination of material and spiritual influences; laying the foundations of success. Reward follows effort.

REVERSED MEANING
Over caution leads to missed opportunities; unwillingness or inability to take help and advice when offered; narrow-mindedness.

FOUR OF DISCS

THE CARD
The ship's captain gives orders to his men. They will soon be setting out to trade with places overseas so all has to be in order.

INTERPRETATION
Starting a project in the right way; careful planning; increase in wealth or influence through trade and peaceful activities.

REVERSED MEANING
Inability to delegate authority; clinging to the old ways; short sightedness; static; avoiding action for fear of loss.

FIVE OF DISCS

THE CARD
The card shows a man and a woman struggling against the wind and snow on a cold winters night. The woman holds a child in her arms and tries to protect it from the cold. In their efforts to combat the elements, both of them risk overlooking the five golden discs that lie partially covered by the falling snow.

INTERPRETATION
Financial troubles, material adversity that needs care to resolve or opportunities may be overlooked; a favourable outcome is available but must not be missed.

REVERSED MEANING
Hard work is needed to overcome problems; improvement could be made through a change in attitude, or by using more imagination.

SIX OF DISCS

THE CARD
The woman sits combing her hair when her husband surprises her with a gift of a golden necklace. he has had success in his trade and shares his good fortune with his wife.

INTERPRETATION
Material gain and profit allow the giving of gifts; helping others; generosity; influence; prosperity; charity.

REVERSED MEANING
Wealth used for purely personal enjoyment and gain; over spending; loss or theft; a reluctance to invest; refusing to help.

SEVEN OF DISCS

THE CARD
The youth sits on the sand dunes staring out to sea. His job is to repair damaged shields but he has no interest in the work. He is happier to just sit and watch the waves breaking on the shore and the gulls gliding effortlessly on the air.

INTERPRETATION
Wasted effort; disinterest and failure; unprofitable use of time; getting behind with work; a lack of commitment.

REVERSED MEANING
Lazy and unenterprising; self-induced financial worries; bankruptcy; gambling.

EIGHT OF DISCS

THE CARD
The craftsman is happy at his work making shields. This has been his life-long trade and he is much respected for his good workmanship.

INTERPRETATION
A steady worker; satisfying and profitable labour; building for the future; planning for retirement.

REVERSED MEANING
Misuse of ones skills; dishonesty in financial affairs; looking for immediate results rather than long-term investment.

NINE OF DISCS

THE CARD
A richly-dressed woman walks upon the sandy shore. She raises a hand to her face as the sea breeze blows her hair. Before her she sees a casket left behind by the tide, containing golden coins.

INTERPRETATION
Material success; unexpected wealth; inheritance or winnings; good luck, comfort and gain.

REVERSED MEANING
Success resulting in the misfortune of others; receiving stolen goods; theft or embezzlement.

TEN OF DISCS

THE CARD
As the sun sets, a wealthy man watches over the sea. The sea was his life. It has given him all he has, and all that he ever needed. He need work no more, nor risk his life on the waves, for now in his old age he is prosperous and content.

INTERPRETATION
Prosperity and material security; family wealth founded on the labours of ones ancestors; inheritance.

REVERSED MEANING
Problems over inheritance; family disagreements over money; dilution of wealth by sharing between many claiments.

PRINCE OF DISCS

THE CARD
The Prince is dressed in the green and brown of the earth.
Over his shoulder is his shield representing the element of
earth. Behind him are the stone remains of a burial mound,
the last resting place of man.

INTERPRETATION
A hard-working and careful person; a good organizer and
administrator; honesty; kindness.

REVERSED MEANING
A poor planner; wasteful and impractical; enjoys the power
of his position; idle; has an overdeveloped sense of his own
importance.

PRINCESS OF DISCS

THE CARD
The Princess contemplates the shield she holds before her.
It symbolizes the element earth, as does the circle of
standing stones in the background.

INTERPRETATION
Practical but unimaginative; hard working; a lover of
traditional values; may be unable to think for herself,
dependent on others for leadership.

REVERSED MEANING
Fighting against progress; lacking foresight; mistrusts
change; unadventurous; interfering.

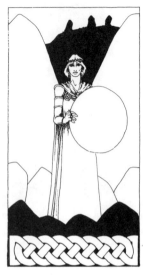

QUEEN OF DISCS

THE CARD
The Queen is surrounded by stone, all positioned by the hand of man. Behind her a hill is surmounted by three standing stones. Her colour is green.

INTERPRETATION
Generous and forgiving; a sensible down-to-earth woman but a lover of comfort, splendour and personal luxury.

REVERSED MEANING
Unintelligent, dull, selfish, will not part with money unless to her own material benefit.

KING OF DISCS

THE CARD
The King holds his shield high above his head. Behind him a rocky outcrop has become overgrown with grass and trees.

INTERPRETATION
A reliable man both steady and methodical; cautious; taking time to come to a decision; patient.

REVERSED MEANING
Materialistic; grasping; insensitive to change; dull-witted and slow; ignorant of art and beauty.

CHAPTER 4

TAROT SPREADS

HOW TO USE THE TAROT CARDS

There are many Tarot spreads to choose from. Some are suitable for questions requiring a simple yes or no answer. This might involve taking a single card and interpreting it in the context of the question. This provides an answer, but not of any great depth. At the other extreme however, spreads can involve the use of the whole deck. These tend to be impractical and over complicated, demanding a great deal of skill from the reader and a fair degree of patience from the questioner. The spreads described below have been chosen for their ease of use and the depth of answer that they can impart.

The first uses four cards and will give a reasonably detailed answer to a simply phrased question. It may be used with ease by the beginner with a minimum knowledge of the Tarot.

The *Four Card Spread* may be of further use as a part of a longer reading using another spread. If some difficulty is pointed out regarding a specific part of the questioner's life, he or she may propose a certain line of remedial action and ask if this would be effective in countering the problem. Then the reader would consult the *Four Card Spread*, and give an answer to this secondary question, without interrupting the flow of the existing spread.

The second is known as the *Celtic Cross Spread*. It is perhaps the most widely used and most popular of all Tarot spreads. Different readers may use slightly different versions but essentially they are the same. The *Celtic Cross Spread* will give the questioner a much more detailed view of his or her circumstances than the *Four*

Card Spread but is still straightforward to use.

The reader should attempt to read the cards in relation to each other. A card in one part of the spread, taken in isolation, may fail to make any sense at all but it will be found that other cards in the spread will support it and give an indication as to how it should be interpreted. Events indicated in the future will often be related in some way to elements of the past. All the cards taken together will provide more meaning than the sum of their individual parts.

The third spread is based on the attributes of the 12 astrological houses. These are simple to understand, dealing as they do with the main spheres of action and concern in a persons life. These areas may be widened to accommodate the individual card if no immediate sense is apparent. If, for instance, a Court card is found in the ninth house, which governs travel, philosophy, etc., it may indicate the questioner's attitude to travel or philosophy, but if the card contradicts what is known about the questioner then another interpretation should be sought. In this case the card could also refer to a travelling companion or perhaps someone offering spiritual guidance. Reference to the other cards of the *Astrological Spread* or to the questioner will show the reader which line to follow.

Both the *Celtic Cross Spread* and the *Astrological Spread* may be expanded quite easily to give a much more detailed reading. First a standard reading is given from the cards as they are, then two further spreads are dealt on top of the first. This will give three cards in each position. From the

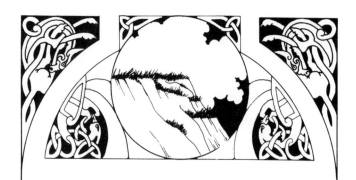

combined reading of each group of three a much greater depth of meaning may be found. Items that made no apparent sense in the first reading will now fall into place within the context of the three cards.

THE CARDS

Tarot reading is a most personal affair. A deck of Tarot cards should be handled as little as possible by anyone other than their owner. Obviously during a reading they have to be given to the questioner to shuffle and cut, but no other handling should be permitted.

Some clairvoyants keep their cards wrapped in silk of various colours, others prefer a good strong wooden box, believing that only natural materials will allow the cards to breathe. Some have their cards in both a silk cloth *and* a box — others neither. Ultimatly it is a matter of personal choice, but some consideration should be made for the protection of the cards, if only to avoid loss or prevent physical damage.

THE READING

The secret of successful reading is practice. Without practice you cannot hope to become a good Tarot Card reader unless

you have, as some do, natural mediumistic abilities.

Use the cards every day if possible. Become familiar with the illustrations then their interpretations. If you have time for nothing else try at least to handle them regularly preferably just before you go to sleep at night. This will allow their content to sink into your subconscious.

Once you have a basic understanding of the cards try the different spreads. Do not be put off if you cannot remember all the meanings; look them up. Keep this book by your side whenever you intend to practice. Make notes of the interpretations using your own words and ideas to expand on those given here. After a time you will find that you do not need the assistance of this book or your notes.

Having mastered the cards try developing the spreads and invent your own. Consult other books on the Tarot and those about divination in general. Absorb what they have to offer; use whatever you can. But do not be held back by them. What one author explains as being absolutely essential another will disregard as irrelevent. Make up your own mind. Develop your use of the Tarot the way you wish and let your inner feelings guide you.

SPREADS

The deck of cards is passed face downwards to the questioner, who should be given the following instructions:

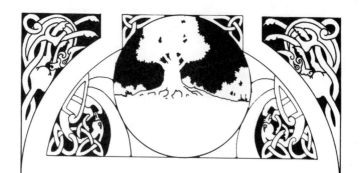

1. Shuffle the cards.
2. Cut the deck into three piles.
3. Take the middle pile and turn it round (to give reversed cards).
4. Place the reversed pile onto the third, and place the first pile on top.
5. Shuffle the cards a second time.
6. Finally cut them and place the bottom pile onto the top.

Take the cards back and begin the spread of your choice.

If the questioner has difficulty handling the cards (they may be too large for some hands) the shuffle may be performed by spreading the whole deck across the table, swirling and mixing them as you would dominoes, then collecting them together and continuing as before.

Some people prefer to use only the Major Arcana for readings. While this may be appealing to the beginner, the temptation should be resisted. At best such a reading would have little value when compared to using the full deck, and at worst the beginner would be ignoring the larger part of the deck at the most important part of the learning cycle. Use the whole deck from the start. The various interpretations and meanings will fall into place and become clear the more you use them.

THE FOUR CARD SPREAD
This is a simple question and answer spread. The question should be phrased in a straightforward manner, without any additional qualifying conditions, following the general line of 'What will happen if . . .?'

Diagram 1 FOUR CARD SPREAD

The event being considerd may be something beyond the questioner's control; perhaps something that will happen anyway, such as 'Will I enjoy my holiday?' where going on holiday is not in doubt. Or it may be something the questioner is thinking of doing, for example 'Should I go on holiday?' Above all the questions should be precise.

The questioner should be asked to concentrate on the question while shuffling the cards. On taking back the cards from the top of the deck deal four cards face uppermost.

The first card describes the overall event, the nature of the action being considered.

The second card represents the effect of the action upon the questioner — what he will think or feel about it.

The third card shows how the questioner will respond to the event being considered — what they will do or not do.

The fourth card gives an idea of the questioner's position

after the event has passed — emotional state; what she gained or lost.

EXAMPLE READING
After hearing about an interesting job vacancy, the unemployed questioner wonders what would follow if he was to apply for the position.

The four cards are:
1. The Seven of Discs
2. The Eight of Wands
3. The Wheel of Fortune
4. The Sun

Diagram 2 EXAMPLE OF FOUR CARD SPREAD

The Seven of Discs shows that the questioner fears that the job being applied for would tie him down, restricting his present state of freedom, but accepts that this may be beneficial.

The second card, the Eight of Wands, indicates that the immediate effect of the application upon the questioner will be a message requiring, or possibly for the job itself — something which may cause a little panic.

The Wheel of Fortune suggests that the questioner will respond well to the call for action, adapting comfortably to the feared changes that work will bring. **Rad**, the rune of movement and change, confirms this.

The final card, the Sun, shows that the questioner will be successful in his application and will be happy in his new position (the rune **Winn** is the rune of joy), and also that he will have a much healthier outlook on life in general.

THE CELTIC CROSS
Before passing the deck to the questioner for shuffling, remove a card to represent the questioner. This should be chosen following the method descrbed in Chapter Two. Place this card, the Significator, in the centre of the table and ask the questioner to concentrate on it as the cards are shuffled.
    Lay the cards out as shown in the diagram, following the same order, the first card covering the Significator. The cards are then interpreted in relation to their positions as follows:
1. The inner self; how the questioner likes to see himself and his position in the world.
2. The projected self; other people's view of the questioner. (If the top of this card lies to the right it should be read as being reversed.)

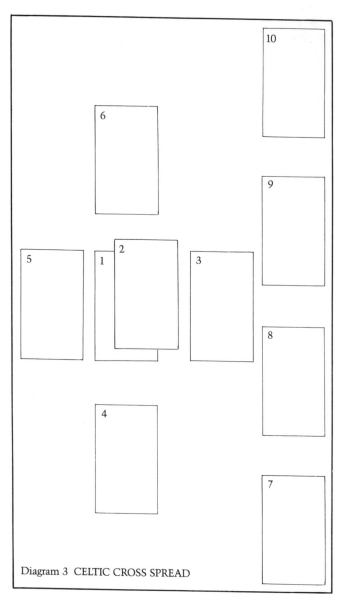

Diagram 3 CELTIC CROSS SPREAD

3. The distant past, old influences, or those that are now fading away, yet are still present and active in some form.
4. The near past, stronger or more recent influences affecting the questioner.
5. Influences or events in the near future.
6. The possible outcome; a future that may occur or may not. The other cards will give an indication of what may be done to achieve or avoid this situation.
7. The self. How the questioner effects his environment; the way in which he interacts with others.
8. The environment. How the questioner's surroundings influence him.
9. Hopes. This may also indicate the questioner's fears, depending on the card.
10. The outcome. As things stand at the time of the reading this card indicates what will happen in the future.

EXAMPLE READING
A card is chosen to represent the questioner. As the questioner in this case was a man nearing retirement, a King was chosen. He was born under the sign of Aries, so it was the King of Wands.

The cards were shuffled, and dealt around the Significator in the following manner:

1. The World
2. Queen of Cups
3. Six of Wands
4. Ace of Cups, reversed

Diagram 4 EXAMPLE OF CELTIC CROSS SPREAD

5. Princess of Wands
6. Eight of Discs, reversed
7. Ace of Swords
8. Four of Cups
9. Two of Wands
10. The Empress

The World in the first position shows that internally the questioner feels that he has been successful and is now ready to move on to other things; he has finished one era and wishes to go on to the next.

The Queen of Cups indicates that he presents the world with an image of being of an artistic temperament but perhaps with a tendency to be a dreamer and not of strong character.

The Six of Wands shows achievements in the past which, from the Ace of Cups reversed, lead to a period of some contentment.

The Princess of Wands in the fifth position suggests that at some time in the near future he will be influenced by an impulsive restless person who may well become an important, if disruptive, part of his life.

In the sixth position, that of the possible outcome, the Eight of Discs is inverted — a warning that if the questioner becomes too impatient with his rate of progress he may be tempted to use dishonest means to achieve his aims.

The Ace of Swords, in the seventh position, links in with the World and the Six of Wands, repeating that he is satisfied

with what has happened in the past and is looking eagerly for ways to move on.

The Four of Cups suggests that things are not moving quickly enough for him. He feels that he is being held back by something or someone and is dissatisfied with his rate of progress.

The Two of Wands indicates that he expects his previous successes to continue in the future but realizes that they will only be won through hard work.

The final card is the Empress, a card of growth, abundance, happiness and stability. If he can resist the temptation to speed his progress by underhand methods he will in the end succeed in his ambitions.

THE ASTROLOGICAL SPREAD
This spread, as its name implies, is based upon the principles of astrology. 12 cards are placed in positions representing the 12 astrological houses. Each card is interpreted within the context of the individual house. This may take a little longer to learn for the beginner but anyone with a knowledge of astrology will find the principle straightforward.

The cards should be shuffled as described above and the top 12 cards dealt face upwards onto the table. The 12 positions or houses are as follows:

1. The questioner; individuality; identity; physical body.
2. Money and possessions; material things of life; financial stability.

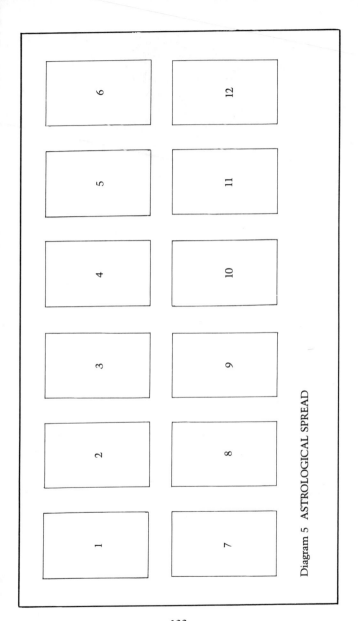

Diagram 5 ASTROLOGICAL SPREAD

3. Education; communication; interests; brothers and sisters.
4. The home and family; origins and roots; the influence of the mother.
5. Leisure activities; creativeness; talents; love and romance; holidays.
6. Work and employment; personal health; employees and dependants.
7. Personal relationships; marriage; partnerships; friends and enemies.
8. Birth and death; beginnings and endings.
9. Travel; philosophy; religion; education.
10. Career; ambitions; achievements.
11. Friends and social life; hopes and wishes.
12. The subconscious; internal thoughts; psychic powers.

EXAMPLE SPREAD
No significator being needed, the cards were shuffled and dealt face up as follows.

First House.	Ace of Swords
Second House.	Princess of Cups
Third House.	The World
Fourth House.	The Hanged Man
Fifth House.	Three of Wands, reversed
Sixth House.	The Chariot
Seventh House.	Queen of Cups
Eighth House.	The Tower, reversed
Ninth House.	The Empress, reversed
Tenth House.	Nine of Cups

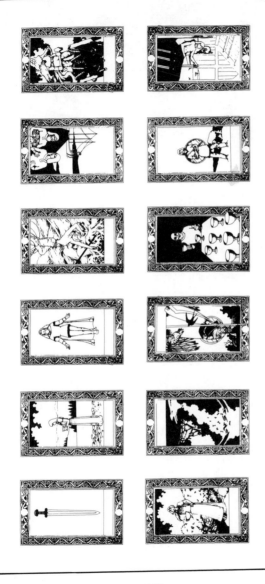

Diagram 6 EXAMPLE OF ASTROLOGICAL SPREAD

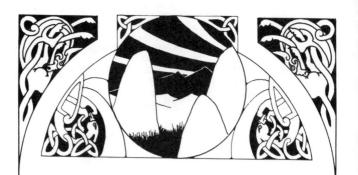

| Eleventh House. | Prince of Discs |
| Twelfth House. | Four of Swords, reversed |

The Ace of Swords in the first house shows that the questioner is an intellectual type; he enjoys new ideas and loves change.

The Princess of Cups in the second house indicates that he is able to gain financially from the use of his mind — perhaps he is a teacher or an instructor of some kind, but he may tend to become bored through a lack of mental stimulus.

In the third house lies The World, signifying educational success and achievement. This person has a substantial number of academic qualifications behind him, but the rune **Mann** suggests that he uses his skills to benefit others.

The Hanged Man, in the fourth house, indicates that to achieve his educational success he may have had to forgo or restrict his links with his home, family or friends, perhaps living away for a lengthy period. Or maybe he was unable to settle down to family life due to his commitments. His educational links are re-enforced by the rune **Os**.

This commitment, as seen in the reversed Three of Wands, has also led to the rejection of leisure interests as most people would see them. He considers his work to be the source of his relaxation, he is devoted to his profession.

The Chariot shows that he is in full control of his circumstances. His life may be dominated by his work but

it is of his own choosing. The rune **Thorn** shows that he feels secure in his present position.

Despite his sound logical judgement in personal relationships, he is prone to let his heart rule his mind, as may be observed from the Queen of Cups in the seventh house.

In the eighth house the Tower is reversed denoting that he tends to worry unnecessarily about the future. Perhaps he fears, as the rune **Hagall** suggests, the loss of security that he at present enjoys in his position at work.

The ninth card, the Empress reversed, points to a feminine influence that is, or has been, restrictive in some way. This may have resulted from his leaving home when younger, perhaps he has a feeling of guilt at leaving his mother. The rune **Ger** suggests that this restriction has not proved unfruitful and may well have a bearing upon his overall success.

He is however satisfied with his achievements. He has done well and he knows this, as the Nine of Cups in the position of careers relates.

The princess of Discs in the eleventh house shows that he treats his friends and associates with the same degree of care and commitment as he does the rest of his life.

The reversed Four of Swords is connected to the previous card. The card suggests that as he fears isolation, he cultivates his friendships with great care. Perhaps he has

visions of being left alone in his later years. His time away from his family may have led him to fear loss of contact with people and may also explain his emotional encounters with women. The questioner should come to terms with the past; he is successful and has a bright future ahead of him.

TABLES OF CORRESPONDENCES IN THE MAJOR ARCANA

1. CARDS

No.	Card	Picture	Attribution or symbolism
0	Fool	Balder	Sun, purity
1	Magician	Odin	Knowledge, magic runes
2	High priestess	Frigga	Divination, womanhood
3	Empress	Freya	Love, beauty, fertility
4	Emperor	Tyr	War, protection
5	High priest	Frey	Peace, prosperity
6	Lovers	Brisingaman	Necklace of the dwarfs
7	Chariot	Thor	Sky, thunder
8	Justice	Forseti	Wisdom, law
9	Hermit	Heimdall	Watchman
10	Wheel	Norns	Past, present, future
11	Strength	Tyr	Binding of Fenris
12	Hanged Man	Odin	Sacrifice for knowledge
13	Death	Honir	Silence
14	Temperance	Hel	Underworld
15	Devil	Loki	Malevolent fire
16	Tower	Ragnarok	Twilight of the gods
17	Star	Star	Hope
18	Moon	Moon	Son of Mani
19	Sun	Sun	Daughter of Sol
20	Judgement	New gods	Sons of the gods
21	World	Balder	Rebirth

2. RUNES

No.	*Rune name*	*Rune*	*Interpretation*
0	Sigil	ᛋ	Glittering, sun
1	Peorth	ᛕ	Dice cup
2	Ear	ᛠ	Sea, water
3	Ger	ᛃ	Year, harvest
4	Tir	ᛏ	Splendour, power, glory
5	Ing	ᛝ	One who travels in a wagon
6	Gyfu	ᚷ	Gift
7	Thorn	ᚦ	Thor
8	Lagu	ᛚ	What is laid or fixed, the law
9	Eolh	ᛉ	Protection
10	Rad	ᚱ	Riding, travel, knowledge
11	Ur	ᚢ	Trials of strength
12	Os	ᚩ	God, hero, Odin
13	Yr	ᛇ	Yew tree, death
14	Beorc	ᛒ	Rebirth, spring
15	Nyd	ᚾ	Neid, Thralldom
16	Hagall	ᚺ	Hail
17	Cen	ᚲ	Torch
18	Is	ᛁ	Ice, winter
19	Winn	ᚹ	Joy
20	Ethel	ᛟ	Inheritance, homeland
21	Mann	ᛗ	Mankind

3. HEBREW LETTERS

No.	Hebrew	Letter	Meaning	Astrological
0	Aleph	א	Ox	Air
1	Beth	ב	House	Mercury
2	Gimel	ג	Camel	Moon
3	Daleth	ד	Door	Venus
4	Tzaddi	צ	Fish hook	Aries
5	Vau	ו	Nail	Taurus
6	Zain	ז	Sword	Gemini
7	Cheth	ח	Fence	Cancer
8	Lamed	ל	Ox goad	Libra
9	Yod	י	Hand	Virgo
10	Kaph	כ	Palm	Jupiter
11	Teth	ט	Serpent	Leo
12	Mem	מ	Water	Water
13	Nun	נ	Fish	Scorpio
14	Samekh	ס	Prop	Sagittarius
15	A'ain	ע	Eye	Capricorn
16	Pe	פ	Mouth	Mars
17	He	ה	Window	Aquarius
18	Qoph	ק	Back of head	Pisces
19	Resh	ר	Head	Sun
20	Shin	ש	Tooth	Fire
21	Tau	ת	Tau cross	Saturn

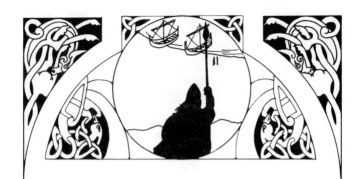

NOTES

0. The Fool card carries the rune **Sigil,** meaning glittering or sun. The illustration is of the god Balder, known as 'the Bright'. He is the innocent god of the sun, a virtuous god loved by all the other gods of the Aesir.
1. The Magician, Odin the Trickster. The rune **Peorth,** meaning dice cup, is used to symbolize the uncertainty of his allegiances.
2. The High Priestess is traditionally associated with the moon and water. Often the image of the High Priestess is modelled on a traditional visual conception of the Virgin Mary, the name Mary being derived from 'mer' meaning sea, qabalistically Binah; all of which are associated with the rune, **Ear.** Also the rune can be interpreted as 'before'. Frigga is the goddess of divination.
3. The Empress, the rune **Ger**, symbolizes the year and the harvest, the cyclic nature of natural progression. Freya is the Nordic fertility goddess, the goddess of plenty.
4. The Emperor, the rune **Tir.** The rune of the god Tyr symbolizes splendour, power, brightness and glory.
5. The rune **Ing**, is interpreted as 'one who travels on a wagon', which is generally accepted as referring to the god Frey, who was represented in a seated position suggesting the traditional image of the Hierophant, and accompanied by attendant priests.
6. The Lovers. Freya is the wife of Odin; she is the goddess of fertility; the Empress. She has to choose either to

remain faithful to Odin or to sleep with the dwarfs and receive in turn the necklace she longs for. The rune **Gyfu**, is interpreted as 'gift'. The necklace is a gift if she wishes it, but the true gift, as was given to Eve in the Garden of Eden, is the gift of choice, faithfulness or desire.

7. The Chariot. Thor rides in his celestial chariot drawn by two black goats. The rune is **Thorn**, the rune of Thor.

8. Justice; illustrated with the figure of Forseti, the law giver to the gods. The rune **Lagu**, is defined as 'what is laid or fixed. The Law'.

9. The Hermit is Heimdal. With his horn he watches over the rainbow bridge, Bifrost, the gateway to Asgard. He stands alone in the wilderness of ice. He is the watchman, the guardian of the gods, as indicated by the rune **Eolh** — protection.

10. The Wheel of Fortune is illustrated with the Norns spinning their web of fate and the tree Yggdrasil, which supports the changing world, high within its branches. The rune **Rad**, is the rune of riding and travel. It is a rune of change and motion. It can also be interpreted as knowledge; the knowledge of fate which lies in the hanging web of the Norns.

11. Strength is the god Tyr, the Emperor, seen in the act of binding the wolf Fenris, which none of the other gods are able to do. The rune of this card is **Ur**, meaning 'trials of strength'.

12. The Hanged Man, Odin, the rune **Os**, (related to the rune Aesc), is defined as 'ash trees' and 'ash spear', two of the

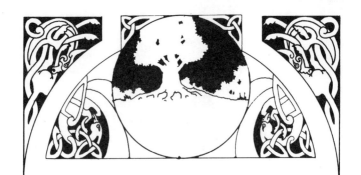

symbols in this card. Odin hangs from the Ash tree, and is wounded by the spear of ash. Also, from the Old English Rune Poem comes the phrase 'Os is the origin of all speech', emphasizing Odin's action; reaching down into the waters of knowledge for the runes of wisdom.

13. Death, blind Hod, unwittingly kills Balder. **Eoh**, the rune of death, also signifies 'horse' which in many Northern cults was a sacrificial animal, thus repeating the sacrificial aspect of Balder's death. Balder is a solar deity, and his return is confidently expected by the other gods. Death is a card of change.

14. Temperance. Hermod rides to Hel the goddess of the underworld, to beg for the life of Balder to be returned. Hel is understanding, and providing a certain condition is met, she is willing to do as Hermod asks. **Beorc** is the rune; its meaning is 'rebirth' or 'spring'. One of the titles of the card is the Bringer Forth of Life.

15. The Devil is Loki who contrives to defeat the gods in their attempt to meet the condition set by Hel, thus denying Balder his freedom from death. The gods discover his treachery and bind him to a rock until the end of the earth. The rune here is **Nyd**, meaning need, or thralldom, symbolizing Loki's position of confinement.

16. The Tower, the rune **Hagall**, is interpreted as 'hail', a condition that could be most severe and was always uncontrollable by man. The card shows Ragnarok, the inescapable end of the gods.

17. The Star, **Cen**, or torch is the light in the darkness, the

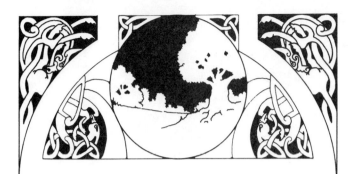

star of hope. As the Star of Bethlehem heralds the coming of Christ, the Morning Star heralds the rising Sun; it is the star of promise shining down on the earth, the land of men.

18. The Moon marks the boundary between heaven and earth. Shining at night it looks over the sleeping earth. The rune **Is** is interpreted as 'ice' and 'winter'. Winter is the season of rest.

19. The Sun is the daughter of Sol, whose mother was Mundilfari. She shines down on the new born earth. The rune is **Winn**, signifying joy.

20. The card Judgement is combined with the rune **Ethel**, meaning 'inheritance' and 'homeland'. It is the card of the new gods born to replace the old ones upon the earth that they inherit.

21. The World shows Balder returned from the land of death to lead the gods and mankind in the new world. The rune born upon this card is **Mann**, meaning 'mankind' or simply 'man'.

THE BORDER
The World Ash, Yggdrasil, surrounds the cards. Nidhogg lurks gnawing amonst the roots, whilst the stags wander about its foliage, nibbling at the young buds. High in the branches the eagle Lerad and the falcon Vedfolnir sit.

CORRESPONDENCES
Due to the vast difference in the traditions involved between the Tarot, the Norse Gods, and the runes, many cards have

multiple, and at times somewhat conflicting correspondences. Therefore the correspondences used have been chosen for their practical attributions and are not to be considered in the ultimate sense, as the final or the only possible associations.

These differences however serve to enhance the interpretations of both the cards and the runes, giving additional dimensions of meaning to both systems, and are especially useful when using the cards as a focus in meditation.

APPENDIX B:

A QUICK GUIDE TO INTERPRETATION

1. THE MAJOR ARCANA

No.	Card	Interpretation
0	Fool	New beginnings, optimism, purity.
1	Magician	Wisdom, communication, information.
2	High Priestess	Insight, hidden knowledge.
3	Empress	Maternal care, fertility.
4	Emperor	A father figure, authority.
5	High Priest	Spiritual leadership, good advice.
6	Lovers	A choice, love, partnerships.
7	Chariot	Progress, firm control, good health.
8	Justice	Truth, harmony, legal matters.
9	Hermit	Guidance, wisdom, warnings.
10	Wheel	Change, good luck, improvement.
11	Strength	Self discipline, courage, strength.
12	Hanged Man	Voluntary sacrifice, initiation.
13	Death	A turning point, transformation.
14	Temperance	Co-operation, balance, optimism.
15	Devil	Temptation, a need for control.
16	Tower	Sudden changes, conflict, release.
17	Star	A bright future, hope.
18	Moon	Dreams, illusion, escapism.
19	Sun	Happiness, joy, good fortune.
20	Judgement	Awakening, positive action.
21	World	Completion, fulfilment, success.

2. THE MINOR ARCANA

Suits	General Interpretation
Wands	Actions, achievements.
Cups	Emotions, relationships.
Swords	The mind, difficulties.
Discs	Money, possessions.

Cards	Interpretation
Ace	New beginnings, births
2	Partnerships, relationships.
3	Foundations, planning.
4	Rest, stability.
5	Setbacks, losses.
6	Gains, triumphs.
7	Care, perseverance.
8	Changes, movement.
9	Security, satisfaction.
10	Success, completion.
Prince	Young males, reliable.
Princess	Young females, active.
Queen	Older females, motherly.
King	Older males, authoritative.

BIBLIOGRAPHY

TAROT

Cavendish, Richard, *The Tarot*, Chancellor Press, London, 1986

Connolly, Eileen, *Tarot: a New Handbook for the Apprentice*, Newcastle Publishing Company, California, 1979.

Crowley, Aleister, *Tarot Divination*, Samuel Weiser, New York, 1976

—— *The Book of Thoth*, Samuel Weiser, New York 1974.

Douglas, Alfred, *The Tarot*, Penguin, 1977.

Fenton, Sasha, *Fortune-Telling by Tarot Cards*, Aquarian Press, Wellingborough, 1985

—— *Tarot in Action!*, Aquarian Press, Wellingborough, 1987

Hudson, Paul, *The Devil's Picture Book*, Abacus, London, 1977

Kaplan, Stuart, R. *The Classical Tarot*, Aquarian Press, Wellingborough, 1984.

—— *Tarot Cards for Fun and Fortune-Telling*, Aquarian Press, Wellingborough, 1986

—— *The Encylopedia of Tarot*, Two Volumes, US Games Systems, New York, vol 1 1985, vol 2 1986

Knight, Gareth, *The Treasure House of Images*, Aquarian Press, Wellingborough, 1986

Mathers, S.L. MacGregor, *The Tarot*, Samuel Weiser, New York

Nichols, Sallie, *Jung and the Tarot*, Samuel Weiser, New York, 1984

Ouspensky, P.D., *The Symbolism of the Tarot*, Dover, New York, 1976

Peach, Emily, *The Tarot Workbook*, Aquarian Press, Wellingborough, 1984

—— *Tarot for Tomorrow*, Aqurian Press, Wellingborough, 1988

Pollack, Rachel, *The New Tarot*, Aquarian Press, Wellingborough, 1989
—— *Seventy-Eight Degrees of Wisdom, Parts 1 & 2*, Aquarian Press, Wellingborough, 1980, 1983
Shephard, John, *The Tarot Trumps, Cosmos in Minature*, Aquarian Press, Wellingborough, 1985
Waite, Arthur Edward, *The Pictorial Key to the Tarot*, Rider, London, 1978
Wang, Robert, *An Introduction to the Golden Dawn Tarot*, Samuel Weiser, New York, 1978
Wirth, Oswald, *The Tarot of the Magicians*, Samuel Weiser, New York, 1985.

THE RUNES
Blum, Ralph, *The Book of Runes*, Michael Joseph, London, 1982
Howard, Michael, *The Runes*, Aquarian Press, Wellingborough, 1978
—— *The Wisdom of the Runes*, Rider, London, 1985
Peterson, James, M., *The Enchanted Alphabet*, Aquarian Press, Wellingborough, 1989.
Thorsson, Edred, *Futhark*, Aquarian Press, Wellingborough, 1984.
Willis, Tony, *The Runic Workbook*, Aquarian Press, Wellingborough, 1984.

MYTHOLOGY AND HISTORY
Arbman, Holger, *The Vikings*, Thames & Hudson, London, 1962

Barrett, Clive, *The Gods of Asgard*, Aquarian Press, Wellingborough, 1989

Bosworth, Joseph, *Anglo-Saxon Dictionary*, John Russell Smith, London, 1852

Branston, Brian, *Gods of the North*, Thames and Hudson, London, 1980

—— *The Lost Gods of England*, Thames and Hudson, London, 1957

Brown, David, *Anglo-Saxon England*, Bodley Head, London, 1978

Chadwick, H.M., *The Cult of Othin*, C.J. Clay & Sons, London, 1899

Crossley-Holland, Kevin, *The Norse Myths*, Andre Deutsch, London, 1980

Davison, H.R. Ellis, *Gods and Myths of Northern Europe*, Penguin, 1979 *Scandanavian Mythology*, Paul Hamlyn, London, 1969

Dronke, U. (ed), *The Poetic Edda*, Oxford University Press, London, 1969

Klindt-Jensen, Ole, *A History of Scandinavian Archaeology*, Thames and Hudson, London, 1975

Magnusson, Magnus & Forman, Werner, *Viking*, Orbis, London, 1979

Owen, Gale R., *Rites and Religions of the Anglo-Saxons*, David and Charles, London, 1981

Page, R.I., *Runes*, British Museum Publications, London, 1987

Percy, Bishop (trans), *Malet's Northern Antiquities*, Bell & Daldy, London, 1873

Seebohm, Frederic, *Tribal Custom in Anglo-Saxon Law*, Longmans, Green and Co. London, 1902

Wilson, David M. (ed), *The Northern World*, Thames and Hudson, London, 1980

Wood, Michael, In *Search of the Dark Ages*, BBC, London, 1981

SYMBOLISM

Cooper, J.C., *Symbolism*, Aquarian Press, Wellingborough, 1985

—— *An Illustrated Encyclopeadia of Traditional Symbols*, Thames & Hudson, London, 1982

Crowley, Aleister, *777 and other Qabalistic Writings*, Samuel Weiser, New York, 1977

Freeman, Martin, *How to interpret a Birth Chart*, Aquarian Press, Wellingborough, 1981

Gettings, Fred, *Dictionary of Occult, Hermetic and Alchemical Symbols*, Routledge & Kegan Paul, London, 1979

—— *Encyclopedia of the Occult*, Century Hutchinson, London, 1986

Jung, Carl (ed), *Man and His Symbols*, Picador, London, 1979

Koch, Rudolf, *The Book of Signs*, Dover, New York, 1955

Mansall, Cordelia, *The Astrology Workbook*, Aquarian Press, Wellingborough, 1985

Silberer, Herbert, *Hidden Symbolism of Alchemy and the Occult Arts*, Dover, New York, 1971

INDEX

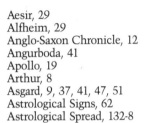

Other recommended
reading . . .

THE NEW TAROT
Modern Variations of Ancient Images
Rachel Pollack

The last 15 years have seen what many people call the
'Tarot Renaissance'. In this book, Rachel Pollack
carefully examines the messages behind all the modern
variations on the ancient Tarot form. Contemporary
designers have used the versatility of Tarot to tailor its
images to their various themes, including storytelling,
humour, spiritual tradition and cultures, psychology,
esotericism, women's spirituality, and astrology —
there is even the monumental 'Tarot Garden' in which
huge sculptures tower over the trees.

Lavishly illustrated, *The New Tarot* looks critically
at over 70 decks produced in the last 15 years, indicating
their strengths and weaknesses and comparing them
with each other and with those traditional decks
which have inspired them.

THE AQUARIAN
RUNE PACK

Anthony Clark, with Tony Willis

This stunning set of 26 rune cards has been based on the symbolism of the Anglo-Saxon runes. Painted by Anthony Clark, the originator and artist of *The Magickal Tarot*, the deck provides the rune-caster with a new and convenient way of practising his or her craft.

The deck is accompanied by Tony Willis's exclusive *The Rune User's Handbook*, a basic introduction to the ancient art of runic divination. Clearly and concisely, the book outlines the background to the rune figures and explains how to cast the runes and interpret the symbolism of the cards.

Together, the two provide a unique method of learning the magic of the runes.

THE MERLIN TAROT

R. J. Stewart
Illustrated by Miranda Gray

The Merlin Tarot is a unique Tarot concept. Based entirely upon the adventures of Merlin, drawn directly from authentic twelfth-century sources, it is a modern restatement of a set of primal, powerful magical images which predates the earliest known set of Tarot cards by over 200 years.

This special pack contains *The Merlin Tarot Deck*, superbly illustrated by Miranda Gray, whose images are unequalled tools for visualization, meditation and prediction, together with *The Merlin Tarot Book*, R. J. Stewart's detailed examination of the cards with the original methods of relating them to cosmology and psychology found in the ancient Merlin texts.

THE ARTHURIAN TAROT

Caitlín and John Matthews
Illustrated by Miranda Gray

The Arthurian Tarot represents the ultimate in Tarot design. Steeped in the sheer unequalled magic of the legends, history and traditions of Arthurian Britain, these exceptional cards capture in 78 frames all the wonder and beauty of King Arthur's realm. Conceived and designed by Caitlín and John Matthews and beautifully executed by Miranda Gray, this original pack reveals the ancient traditions of the Arthurian Mysteries as a living mythos for creative visualization and personal transformation.

This exclusive pack comes complete with *The Arthurian Tarot: A Hallowquest Handbook*, a fully-illustrated guide to the divinatory and archetypal meanings of the cards — the 22 Greater Powers and the 56 Lesser Powers. The suits of Sword, Spear, Grail and Stone, corresponding to the four elements of Western esoteric tradition as well as to the four seasons, empower the reader through the sacred quest for the Hallows. The book also gives original methods for reading and using the Tarot, including the Merlin's Mirror and Excalibur spreads, with sample readings to show their practical significance.